Multithreaded JavaScript
Concurrency Beyond the Event Loop

Thomas Hunter II and Bryan English

Beijing • Boston • Farnham • Sebastopol • Tokyo

Multithreaded JavaScript

by Thomas Hunter II and Bryan English

Published by O'Reilly Media, Inc., 1005 Gravenstein Highway North, Sebastopol, CA 95472.

O'Reilly books may be purchased for educational, business, or sales promotional use. Online editions are also available for most titles (*http://oreilly.com*). For more information, contact our corporate/institutional sales department: 800-998-9938 or *corporate@oreilly.com*.

Acquisitions Editor: Amanda Quinn
Development Editor: Corbin Collins
Production Editor: Daniel Elfanbaum
Copyeditor: Tom Sullivan
Proofreader: nSight, Inc.

Indexer: nSight, Inc.
Interior Designer: David Futato
Cover Designer: Karen Montgomery
Illustrator: Kate Dullea

October 2021:   First Edition

Revision History for the First Edition
2021-09-22:   First Release

See *http://oreilly.com/catalog/errata.csp?isbn=9781098104436* for release details.

978-1-098-10443-6

[LSI]

This book is dedicated to Katelyn and Renée.

Table of Contents

Foreword

The book you're holding now is a fun one. It's a JavaScript book that opens with examples written in C, talks about multithreading with an explicitly single-threaded programming language, provides great examples of how and when to intentionally block the event loop after experts have been telling you for years to never do so, and closes with an excellent list of reasons and caveats about why you might not actually want to use the mechanisms the book describes. More importantly, it's a book that I would consider essential reading for any JavaScript developer no matter where your code is expected to be deployed and run.

When I've worked with companies to help them build more efficient and more performant Node.js and JavaScript applications, I've often had to step back and take the time first to discuss many of the common misconceptions developers have about the programming language. For instance, I once had an engineer with a long history in Java and .NET development argue that creating a new promise in JavaScript was a lot like creating a new thread in Java (it's not), and that promises allow JavaScript to run in parallel (they don't). In a separate conversation someone had created a Node.js application that was spawning over a thousand simultaneous worker threads and wasn't sure why they weren't seeing an expected improvement in performance while testing on a machine that had only eight logical CPU cores. The lesson from these conversations is clear: multithreading, concurrency, and parallelism are still very unfamiliar and difficult topics for a very large percentage of JavaScript developers.

Dealing with these misconceptions is what led directly to me (working with my colleague and fellow Node.js Technical Steering Committee member, Matteo Collina) developing the Broken Promises workshop in which we would lay out the foundations of asynchronous programming in JavaScript—teaching engineering teams how to reason more effectively about the order in which their code would execute and the timing of various events. It also led directly to the development of the Piscina open source project (with fellow Node.js core contributor Anna Henningsen), which provides a best-practice implementation of a worker pool model on top of Node.js worker threads. But those only help with part of the challenge.

In this book, Bryan and Thomas expertly lay out the foundations of multithreaded development in general, and deftly illustrate how the various JavaScript runtimes like web browsers and Node.js enable parallel computing with a programming language that includes no built-in mechanisms to enable it. Because the responsibility for providing multithreading support has fallen on the runtimes, and because there are so many differences between those runtimes, browsers and platforms like Node.js implement multithreading in different ways. Although they share similar APIs, a worker thread in Node.js is really not the same thing as a web worker in a web browser. Support for shared workers, web workers, and service workers is nearly universal across browsers, and worker threads have been in Node.js for several years now, but they are all still a relatively new concept for JavaScript developers. No matter where your JavaScript runs, this book will provide important insight and information. Most importantly, however, the authors take the time to explain exactly why you should care at all about multithreading in your JavaScript applications.

— James Snell,
Node.js Technical Steering Committee Member

Preface

Bryan and I (Thomas) first met during my interview at the San Francisco branch for DeNA, a Japanese mobile game development company. Apparently most of the upper management was going to say no, but after the two of us hung out at a Node.js meetup later that night, Bryan went and convinced them to give me an offer.

While at DeNA, Bryan and I worked on writing reusable Node.js modules so that game teams could build out their game servers, combining components as appropriate to suit the needs of their game. Performance was something we were always measuring, and mentoring game teams on performance was a part of the job; our servers were continuously scrutinized by developers in an industry that traditionally relied upon C++.

The two of us would work together in other capacities as well. Another such role was at a small security startup named Intrinsic where we focused on hardening Node.js apps at such a complete and granular level that I doubt the world will ever see another product like it. Performance tuning was a huge concern for that product as well since customers didn't want to take a hit to their throughput. We spent many hours running benchmarks, poring over flamegraphs, and digging through internal Node.js code. Had the worker threads module been available in all the versions of Node.js that our customers demanded, I have no doubt we would have incorporated it into the product.

We've also worked together in nonemployment capacities as well. NodeSchool SF (*https://oreil.ly/TNS5w*) is one such example wherein we both volunteered to teach others how to use JavaScript and create Node.js programs. We have also spoken at many of the same conferences and meetups.

Both of your authors have a passion for JavaScript and Node.js, and for teaching them to others and eliminating misconceptions. When we realized there was such an extreme lack of documentation about building multithreaded JavaScript applications, we knew what we had to do. This book was born from our desire to not only educate others about the capabilities of JavaScript, but also to help prove that platforms like

Node.js are just as capable as any other when it comes to building performant services that utilize the available hardware.

Target Audience

The ideal reader of this book is an engineer who has been writing JavaScript for a few years, and who doesn't necessarily have experience with writing multithreaded applications or even experience with more traditionally multithreaded languages like C++ or Java. We do include some example C application code, as a sort of multithreaded lingua franca, but it's not something that the reader is expected to be familiar with or even understand.

If you do have experience with such languages, that's great, and this book will help you understand the JavaScript equivalent to the functionality provided by whatever language you may be familiar with. On the other hand, if you've only written code using JavaScript, then this book is also for you. We include information across multiple layers of learning; this includes both low-level API references, high-level patterns, and plenty of technical tangents in between to help fill in any gaps.

Goals

Perhaps the most exuberant goal of this book is to bring knowledge to the community that it's possible to build multithreaded applications using JavaScript. Traditionally, JavaScript code was constrained to a single core, and indeed there are many Twitter threads and forum posts describing the language as such. With a title like *Multithreaded JavaScript*, we hope to completely dispel the notion that JavaScript applications are confined to a single core.

At a more concrete level, the goal is to teach you, the reader, several aspects about writing multithreaded JavaScript applications. By the time you're done reading this book you'll understand the various web worker APIs provided in browsers, their strengths and weaknesses, and when to use which. As far as Node.js goes, you'll understand the worker threads module and how its APIs compare to those in the browser.

The book focuses on two approaches to building multithreaded applications: one using message passing and the other using shared memory. By reading this book you'll understand the APIs used to implement each, when you might want to use one approach or the other, and in which situations they can be combined—and you'll even get your hands dirty with some high-level patterns built upon these approaches.

Conventions Used in This Book

The following typographical conventions are used in this book:

Italic

    Indicates new terms, URLs, email addresses, filenames, and file extensions.

`Constant width`

    Used for program listings, as well as within paragraphs to refer to program elements such as variable or function names, databases, data types, environment variables, statements, and keywords.

`Constant width bold`

    Shows commands or other text that should be typed literally by the user.

`Constant width italic`

    Shows text that should be replaced with user-supplied values or by values determined by context.

    This element signifies a tip or suggestion.

    This element signifies a general note.

    This element indicates a warning or caution.

Using Code Examples

Supplemental material (code examples, exercises, etc.) is available for download at *https://github.com/MultithreadedJSBook/code-samples*.

If you have a technical question or a problem using the code examples, please send email to *bookquestions@oreilly.com*.

This book is here to help you get your job done. In general, if example code is offered with this book, you may use it in your programs and documentation. You do not need to contact us for permission unless you're reproducing a significant portion of the code. For example, writing a program that uses several chunks of code from this book does not require permission. Selling or distributing examples from O'Reilly books does require permission. Answering a question by citing this book and quoting example code does not require permission. Incorporating a significant amount of example code from this book into your product's documentation does require permission.

We appreciate, but generally do not require, attribution. An attribution usually includes the title, author, publisher, and ISBN. For example: "*Multithreaded JavaScript* by Thomas Hunter II and Bryan English (O'Reilly). Copyright 2022 Thomas Hunter II and Bryan English, 978-1-098-10443-6."

If you feel your use of code examples falls outside fair use or the permission given above, feel free to contact us at *permissions@oreilly.com*.

O'Reilly Online Learning

 For more than 40 years, *O'Reilly Media* has provided technology and business training, knowledge, and insight to help companies succeed.

Our unique network of experts and innovators share their knowledge and expertise through books, articles, and our online learning platform. O'Reilly's online learning platform gives you on-demand access to live training courses, in-depth learning paths, interactive coding environments, and a vast collection of text and video from O'Reilly and 200+ other publishers. For more information, visit *http://oreilly.com*.

How to Contact Us

Please address comments and questions concerning this book to the publisher:

O'Reilly Media, Inc.
1005 Gravenstein Highway North
Sebastopol, CA 95472
800-998-9938 (in the United States or Canada)
707-829-0515 (international or local)
707-829-0104 (fax)

We have a web page for this book, where we list errata, examples, and any additional information. You can access this page at *https://oreil.ly/multithreaded-js*.

Email *bookquestions@oreilly.com* to comment or ask technical questions about this book.

For news and information about our books and courses, visit *http://oreilly.com*.

Find us on Facebook: *http://facebook.com/oreilly*.

Follow us on Twitter: *http://twitter.com/oreillymedia*.

Watch us on YouTube: *http://www.youtube.com/oreillymedia*.

Acknowledgments

This book was made possible thanks to the detailed technical reviews provided by the following people:

Anna Henningsen (@addaleax)
> Currently part of the MongoDB Developer Tools team in Germany, Anna has been one of the most active contributors to Node.js core over the last five years, and participated significantly in implementing worker threads for the platform. She is fueled by a passion for Node.js and its community.

Shu-yu Guo (@_shu)
> Shu works on JavaScript implementation and standardization. He is a TC39 delegate, one of the editors of the ECMAScript specification, and the author of the memory model. He currently works on the V8 engine at Google, leading JavaScript language feature implementation and standards. Previously, he has worked at Mozilla and Bloomberg.

Fernando Larrañaga (@xabadu)
> Fernando is an engineer and open source contributor who has been leading JavaScript and Node.js communities for several years both in South America and in the United States. He's currently a senior software engineer at Square and an organizer of NodeSchool SF, and with previous tenures at other major tech companies—such as Twilio and Groupon—he has been developing enterprise-level Node.js and scaling web applications used by millions of users since 2014.

## CHAPTER 1

Introduction

Computers used to be much simpler. That's not to say they were easy to use or write code for, but conceptually there was a lot less to work with. PCs in the 1980s typically had a single 8-bit CPU core and not a whole lot of memory. You typically could only run a single program at one time. What we think of these days as operating systems would not even be running at the same time as the program the user was interacting with.

Eventually, people wanted to run more than one program at once, and multitasking was born. This allowed operating systems to run several programs at the same time by switching execution between them. Programs could decide when it would be an appropriate time to let another program run by yielding execution to the operating system. This approach is called *cooperative multitasking*.

In a cooperative multitasking environment, when a program fails to yield execution for any reason, no other program can continue executing. This interruption of other programs is not desirable, so eventually operating systems moved toward *preemptive multitasking*. In this model, the operating system would determine which program would run on the CPU at which time, using its own notion of scheduling, rather than relying on the programs themselves to be the sole deciders of when to switch execution. To this day, almost every operating system uses this approach, even on multi-core systems, because we generally have more programs running than we have CPU cores.

Running multiple tasks at once is extremely useful for both programmers and users. Before threads, a single program (that is, a single *process*) could not have multiple tasks running at the same time. Instead, programmers wishing to perform tasks concurrently would either have to split up the task into smaller chunks and schedule them inside the process or run separate tasks in separate processes and have them communicate with each other.

Even today, in some high-level languages the appropriate way to run multiple tasks at once is to run additional processes. In some languages, like Ruby and Python, there's a *global interpreter lock (GIL)*, meaning only one thread can be executing at a given time. While this makes memory management far more practical, it makes multithreaded programming not as attractive to programmers, and instead multiple processes are employed.

Until fairly recently, JavaScript was a language where the only multitasking mechanisms available were splitting tasks up and scheduling their pieces for later execution, and in the case of Node.js, running additional processes. We'd typically break code up into asynchronous units using callbacks or promises. A typical chunk of code written in this manner might look something like Example 1-1, breaking up the operations by callbacks or `await`.

Example 1-1. A typical chunk of asynchronous JavaScript code, using two different patterns

```
readFile(filename, (data) => {
  doSomethingWithData(data, (modifiedData) => {
    writeFile(modifiedData, () => {
      console.log('done');
    });
  });
});

// or

const data = await readFile(filename);
const modifiedData = await doSomethingWithData(data);
await writeFile(filename);
console.log('done');
```

Today, in all major JavaScript environments, we have access to threads, and unlike Ruby and Python, we don't have a GIL making them effectively useless for performing CPU-intensive tasks. Instead, other trade-offs are made, like not sharing Java-Script objects across threads (at least not directly). Still, threads are useful to JavaScript developers for cordoning off CPU-intensive tasks. In the browser, there are also special-purpose threads that have feature sets available to them that are different from the main thread. The details of how we can do this are the topics of later chapters, but to give you an idea, spawning a new thread and handling a message in a browser can be as simple as Example 1-2.

Example 1-2. Spawning a browser thread

```
const worker = new Worker('worker.js');
worker.postMessage('Hello, world');

// worker.js
self.onmessage = (msg) => console.log(msg.data);
```

The purpose of this book is to explore and explain JavaScript threads as a programming concept and tool. You'll learn how to use them and, more importantly, when to use them. Not every problem needs to be solved with threads. Not even every CPU-intensive problem needs to be solved with threads. It's the job of software developers to evaluate problems and tools to determine the most appropriate solutions. The aim here is to give you another tool and enough knowledge around it to know when to use it and how.

What Are Threads?

In all modern operating systems, all units of execution outside the kernel are organized into processes and threads. Developers can use processes and threads, and communication between them, to add concurrency to a project. On systems with multiple CPU cores, this also means adding parallelism.

When you execute a program, such as Node.js or a code editor, you're initiating a process. This means that code is loaded into a memory space unique to that process, and no other memory space can be addressed by the program without asking the kernel either for more memory or for a different memory space to be mapped in. Without adding threads or additional processes, only one *instruction* is executed at a time, in the appropriate order as prescribed by the program code. If you're unfamiliar, you can think of instructions as a single unit of code, like a line of code. (In fact, an instruction generally corresponds to one line in your processor's assembly code!)

A program may spawn additional processes, which have their own memory space. These processes do not share memory (unless it's mapped in via additional system calls) and have their own instruction pointers, meaning each one can be executing a different instruction at the same time. If the processes are being executed on the same core, the processor may switch back and forth between processes, temporarily stopping execution for that one process while another one executes.

A process may also spawn threads, rather than full-blown processes. A thread is just like a process, except that it shares memory space with the process that it belongs to. A process can have many threads, and each one has its own instruction pointer. All the same properties about execution of processes apply to threads as well. Because they share a memory space, it's easy to share program code and other values between threads. This makes them more valuable than processes for adding concurrency to programs, but at the cost of some complexity in programming, which we'll cover later on in this book.

A typical way to take advantage of threads is to offload CPU-intensive work, like mathematical operations, to an additional thread or pool of threads while the main thread is free to interact externally with the user or other programs by checking for new interactions inside an infinite loop. Many classic web server programs, such as Apache, use a system like this to handle large loads of HTTP requests. This might end up looking something like Figure 1-1. In this model, HTTP request data is passed to a worker thread for processing, and when the response is ready, it's handed back to the main thread to be returned back to the user agent.

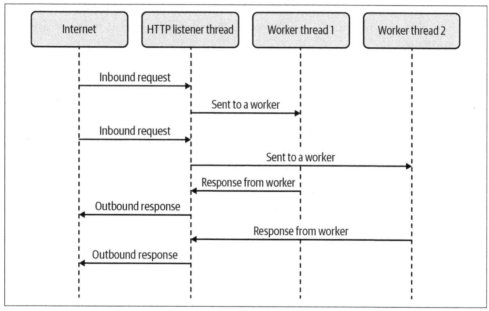

Figure 1-1. Worker threads as they might be used in an HTTP server

In order for threads to be useful, they need to be able to coordinate with each other. This means they have to be able to do things like wait for things to happen on other threads and get data from them. As discussed, we have a shared memory space between threads, and with some other basic primitives, systems for passing messages between threads can be constructed. In many cases, these sorts of constructs are available at the language or platform level.

Concurrency Versus Parallelism

It's important to distinguish between concurrency and parallelism, since they'll come up fairly often when programming in a multithreaded manner. These are closely related terms that can mean very similar things depending on the circumstances. Let's start with some definitions.

Concurrency
> Tasks are run in overlapping time.

Parallelism
> Tasks are run at exactly the same time.

While it may seem like these mean the same thing, consider that tasks may be broken up into smaller parts and then interleaved. In this case, concurrency can be achieved without parallelism because the time frames that the tasks run in can be overlapped. For tasks to be running with parallelism, they must be running at *exactly the same time*. Generally, this means they must be running on separate CPU cores at exactly the same time.

Consider Figure 1-2. In it, we have two tasks running in parallel and concurrently. In the concurrent case, only one task is being executed at a given time, but throughout the entire period, execution switched between the two tasks. This means they're running in overlapping time, so it fits the definition of concurrency. In the parallel case, both tasks are executing simultaneously, so they're running in parallel. Since they're *also* running in an overlapping time period, they're also running concurrently. Parallelism is a subset of concurrency.

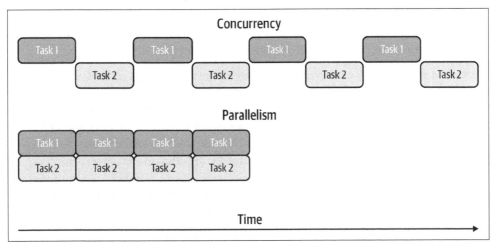

Figure 1-2. Concurrency versus parallelism

Threads do not automatically provide parallelism. The system hardware must allow for this by having multiple CPU cores, and the operating system scheduler must decide to run the threads on separate CPU cores. On single-core systems, or systems with more threads running than CPU cores, multiple threads may be run on a single CPU concurrently by switching between them at appropriate times. Also, in languages with a GIL like Ruby and Python, threads are explicitly prevented from offering parallelism because only one instruction can be executed at a time throughout the entire runtime.

It's important to also think about this in terms of timing because threads are typically added to a program to increase performance. If your system is only allowing for concurrency due to only having a single CPU core available or being already loaded with other tasks, then there may not be any perceived benefit to using extra threads. In fact, the overhead of synchronization and context-switching between the threads may end up making the program perform even worse. Always measure the performance of your application under the conditions it's expected to run in. That way you can verify whether a multithreaded programming model will actually be beneficial to you.

Single-Threaded JavaScript

Historically, the platforms that JavaScript ran on did not provide any thread support, so the language was thought of as single-threaded. Whenever you hear someone say that JavaScript is single-threaded, they're referring to this historical background and the programming style that it naturally lent itself to. It's true that, despite the title of this book, the language itself does not have any built-in functionality to create threads. This shouldn't be that much of a surprise because it also doesn't have any built-in functionality to interact with the network, devices, or filesystem, or to make any system calls. Indeed, even such basics as setTimeout() aren't actually JavaScript features. Instead environments the virtual machine (VM) is embedded in, such as Node.js or browsers, provide these via environment-specific APIs.

Instead of threads as a concurrency primitive, most JavaScript code is written in an event-oriented manner operating on a single execution thread. As various events like user interactions or I/O happen, they trigger the execution of functions previously set to run upon these events. These functions are typically called *callbacks* and are at the core of how asynchronous programming is done in Node.js and the browser. Even in promises or the async/await syntax, callbacks are the underlying primitive. It's important to recognize that callbacks are not running in parallel, or alongside any other code. When code in a callback is running, that's the only code that's currently running. Put another way, only one call stack is active at any given time.

It's often easy to think of operations happening in parallel, when in fact they're happening concurrently. For example, imagine you want to open three files containing numbers, named *1.txt*, *2.txt*, and *3.txt*, and then add up the results and print them. In Node.js, you might do something like Example 1-3.

Example 1-3. Reading from files concurrently in Node.js

```
import fs from 'fs/promises';

async function getNum(filename) {
  return parseInt(await fs.readFile(filename, 'utf8'), 10);
}

try {
  const numberPromises = [1, 2, 3].map(i => getNum(`${i}.txt`));
  const numbers = await Promise.all(numberPromises);
  console.log(numbers[0] + numbers[1] + numbers[2]);
} catch (err) {
  console.error('Something went wrong:');
  console.error(err);
}
```

To run this code, save it in a file called *reader.js*. Make sure you have text files named *1.txt*, *2.txt*, and *3.txt*, each containing integers, and then run the program with `node reader.js`.

Since we're using `Promise.all()`, we're waiting for all three files to be read and parsed. If you squint a bit, it may even look similar to the `pthread_join()` from the C example later in this chapter. However, just because the promises are being created together and waited upon together doesn't mean that the code resolving them runs at the same time, it just means their time frames are overlapping. There's still only one instruction pointer, and only one instruction is being executed at a time.

In the absence of threads, there's only one JavaScript environment to work with. This means one instance of the VM, one instruction pointer, and one instance of the garbage collector. By one instruction pointer, we mean that the JavaScript interpreter is only executing one instruction at any given time. That doesn't mean we're restricted to one global object though. In both the browser and Node.js, we have realms (*https://oreil.ly/uy7E2*) at our disposal.

Realms can be thought of as instances of the JavaScript environment as provided to JavaScript code. This means that each realm gets its own global object, and all of the associated properties of the global object, such as built-in classes like `Date` and other objects like `Math`. The global object is referred to as `global` in Node.js and `window` in browsers, but in modern versions of both, you can refer to the global object as `globalThis`.

In browsers, each frame in a web page has a realm for all of the JavaScript within it. Because each frame has its own copy of `Object` and other primitives within it, you'll notice that they have their own inheritance trees, and `instanceof` might not work as you expect it to when operating on objects from different realms. This is demonstrated in Example 1-4.

Example 1-4. Objects from a different frame in a browser

```
const iframe = document.createElement('iframe');
document.body.appendChild(iframe);
const FrameObject = iframe.contentWindow.Object; ❶

console.log(Object === FrameObject); ❷
console.log(new Object() instanceof FrameObject); ❸
console.log(FrameObject.name); ❹
```

❶ The global object inside the `iframe` is accessible with the `contentWindow` property.

❷ This returns false, so the `Object` inside the frame is not the same as in the main frame.

❸ `instanceof` evaluates to `false`, as expected since they're not the same `Object`.

❹ Despite all this, the constructors have the same `name` property.

In Node.js, realms can be constructed with the `vm.createContext()` function, as shown in Example 1-5. In Node.js parlance, realms are called Contexts. All the same rules and properties applying to browser frames also apply to Contexts, but in Contexts, you don't have access to any global properties or anything else that might be in scope in your Node.js files. If you want to use these features, they need to be manually passed in to the Context.

Example 1-5. Objects from a new Context in Node.js

```
const vm = require('vm');
const ContextObject = vm.runInNewContext('Object'); ❶

console.log(Object === ContextObject); ❷
console.log(new Object() instanceof ContextObject); ❸
console.log(ContextObject.name); ❹
```

❶ We can get objects from a new context using `runInNewContext`.

❷ This returns false, so as with browser iframes, `Object` inside the context is not the same as in the main context.

❸ Similarly, `instanceof` evaluates to `false`.

❹ Once again, the constructors have the same `name` property.

In any of these realm cases, it's important to note that we still only have one instruction pointer, and code from only one realm is running at a time, because we're still only talking about single-threaded execution.

Hidden Threads

While your JavaScript code may run, at least by default, in a single-threaded environment, that doesn't mean the process running your code is single-threaded. In fact, many threads might be used to have that code running smoothly and efficiently. It's a common misconception that Node.js is a single-threaded process.

Modern JavaScript engines like V8 use separate threads to handle garbage collection and other features that don't need to happen in line with JavaScript execution. In addition, the platform runtimes themselves may use additional threads to provide other features.

In Node.js, `libuv` is used as an OS-independent asynchronous I/O interface, and since not all system-provided I/O interfaces are asynchronous, it uses a pool of worker threads to avoid blocking program code when using otherwise-blocking APIs, such as filesystem APIs. By default, four of these threads are spawned, though this number is configurable via the `UV_THREADPOOL_SIZE` environment variable, and can be up to 1,024.

On Linux systems, you can see these extra threads by using `top -H` on a given process. In Example 1-6, a simple Node.js web server was started, and the PID was noted and passed to `top`. You can see the various V8 and `libuv` threads add up to seven threads, including the one that the JavaScript code runs in. You can try this with your own Node.js programs, and even try changing the `UV_THREADPOOL_SIZE` environment variable to see the number of threads change.

Example 1-6. Output from `top`, showing the threads in a Node.js process

```
$ top -H -p 81862
top - 14:18:49 up 1 day, 23:18,  1 user,  load average: 0.59, 0.82, 0.83
Threads:   7 total,   0 running,   7 sleeping,   0 stopped,   0 zombie
%Cpu(s):  2.2 us,  0.0 sy,  0.0 ni, 97.8 id,  0.0 wa,  0.0 hi,  0.0 si,  0.0 st
MiB Mem :  15455.1 total,   2727.9 free,   5520.4 used,   7206.8 buff/cache
MiB Swap:   2048.0 total,   2048.0 free,      0.0 used.   8717.3 avail Mem

    PID USER      PR  NI    VIRT    RES    SHR S  %CPU  %MEM     TIME+ COMMAND
  81862 bengl     20   0  577084  29272  25064 S   0.0   0.2   0:00.03 node
```

```
81863 bengl    20   0  577084  29272  25064 S   0.0   0.2   0:00.00 node
81864 bengl    20   0  577084  29272  25064 S   0.0   0.2   0:00.00 node
81865 bengl    20   0  577084  29272  25064 S   0.0   0.2   0:00.00 node
81866 bengl    20   0  577084  29272  25064 S   0.0   0.2   0:00.00 node
81867 bengl    20   0  577084  29272  25064 S   0.0   0.2   0:00.00 node
81868 bengl    20   0  577084  29272  25064 S   0.0   0.2   0:00.00 node
```

Browsers similarly perform many tasks, such as Document Object Model (DOM) rendering, in threads other than the one used for JavaScript execution. An experiment with top -H like we did for Node.js would result in a similar handful of threads. Modern browsers take this even further by using multiple processes to add a layer of security by isolation.

It's important to think about these extra threads when going through a resource-planning exercise for your application. You should never assume that just because JavaScript is single-threaded that only one thread will be used by your JavaScript application. For example, in production Node.js applications, measure the number of threads used by the application and plan accordingly. Don't forget that many of the native addons in the Node.js ecosystem spawn threads of their own as well, so it's important to go through this exercise on an application-by-application basis.

Threads in C: Get Rich with Happycoin

Threads are obviously not unique to JavaScript. They're a long-standing concept at the operating system level, independent of languages. Let's explore how a threaded program might look in C. C is an obvious choice here because the C interface for threads is what underlies most thread implementations in higher-level languages, even if there may seem to be different semantics.

Let's start with an example. Imagine a proof-of-work algorithm for a simple and impractical cryptocurrency called Happycoin, as follows:

1. Generate a random unsigned 64-bit integer.
2. Determine whether or not the integer is happy.
3. If it's not happy, it's not a Happycoin.
4. If it's not divisible by 10,000, it's not a Happycoin.
5. Otherwise, it's a Happycoin.

A number is happy if it eventually goes to 1 when replacing it with the sum of the squares of its digits, and looping until either the 1 happens, or a previously seen number arises. Wikipedia defines it clearly (*https://oreil.ly/vRr3P*) and also points out that if any previously seen numbers arise, then 4 will arise, and vice versa. You may notice that our algorithm is needlessly too expensive because we could check for divisibility before checking for happiness. This is intentional because we're trying to demonstrate a heavy workload.

Let's build a simple C program that runs the proof-of-work algorithm 10,000,000 times, printing any Happycoins found, and a count of them.

 The cc in the compilation steps here can be replaced with gcc or clang, depending on which is available to you. On most systems, cc is an alias for either gcc or clang, so that's what we'll use here.

Windows users may have to do some extra work here to get this going in Visual Studio, and the threads example won't work out-of-the-box on Windows because it uses Portable Operating System Interface (POSIX) threads rather than Windows threads, which are different. To simplify trying this on Windows, the recommendation is to use Windows Subsystem for Linux so that you have a POSIX-compatible environment to work with.

With Only the Main Thread

Create a file called *happycoin.c*, in a directory called *ch1-c-threads/*. We'll build up this file over the course of this section. To start off, add the code as shown in Example 1-7.

Example 1-7. ch1-c-threads/happycoin.c

```
#include <inttypes.h>
#include <stdbool.h>
#include <stdio.h>
#include <stdlib.h>
#include <time.h>

uint64_t random64(uint32_t * seed) {
  uint64_t result;
  uint8_t * result8 = (uint8_t *)&result;  ❶
  for (size_t i = 0; i < sizeof(result); i++) {
    result8[i] = rand_r(seed);
  }
  return result;
}
```

❶ This line uses pointers, which may be unfamiliar to you if you're coming from a mostly JavaScript background. The short version of what's going on here is that result8 is an array of eight 8-bit unsigned integers, backed by the same memory as result, which is a single 64-bit unsigned integer.

We've added a bunch of includes, which give us handy things like types, I/O functions, and the time and random number functions we'll be needing. Since the algorithm requires the generation of a random 64-bit unsigned integer (i.e., a uint64_t), we need eight random bytes, which random64() gives us by calling rand_r() until we have enough bytes. Since rand_r() also requires a reference to a seed, we'll pass that into random64() as well.

Now let's add our happy number calculation as shown in Example 1-8.

Example 1-8. ch1-c-threads/happycoin.c

```c
uint64_t sum_digits_squared(uint64_t num) {
  uint64_t total = 0;
  while (num > 0) {
    uint64_t num_mod_base = num % 10;
    total += num_mod_base * num_mod_base;
    num = num / 10;
  }
  return total;
}

bool is_happy(uint64_t num) {
  while (num != 1 && num != 4) {
    num = sum_digits_squared(num);
  }
  return num == 1;
}

bool is_happycoin(uint64_t num) {
  return is_happy(num) && num % 10000 == 0;
}
```

To get the sum of the squares of the digits in sum_digits_squared, we're using the mod operator, %, to get each digit from right to left, squaring it, then adding it to our running total. We then use this function in is_happy in a loop, stopping when the number is 1 or 4. We stop at 1 because that indicates the number is happy. We also stop at 4 because that's indicative of an infinite loop where we never end up at 1. Finally, in is_happycoin(), we do the work of checking whether a number is happy and also divisible by 10,000.

Let's wrap this all up in our main() function as shown in Example 1-9.

Example 1-9. ch1-c-threads/happycoin.c

```c
int main() {
  uint32_t seed = time(NULL);
  int count = 0;
  for (int i = 1; i < 10000000; i++) {
    uint64_t random_num = random64(&seed);
    if (is_happycoin(random_num)) {
```

```
            printf("%" PRIu64 " ", random_num);
            count++;
        }
    }
    printf("\ncount %d\n", count);
    return 0;
}
```

First, we need a seed for the random number generator. The current time is as suitable a seed as any, so we'll use that via time(). Then, we'll loop 10,000,000 times, first getting a random number from random64(), then checking if it's a Happycoin. If it is, we'll increment the count and print the number out. The weird PRIu64 syntax in the printf() call is necessary for properly printing out 64-bit unsigned integers. When the loop completes, we print out the count and exit the program.

To compile and run this program, use the following commands in your *ch1-c-threads* directory.

```
$ cc -o happycoin happycoin.c
$ ./happycoin
```

You'll get a list of Happycoins found on one line and the count of them on the next line. For a given run of the program, it might look something like this:

```
11023541197304510000 ...  [ 167 more entries ] ... 770541398378840000
count 169
```

It takes a nontrivial amount of time to run this program; about 2 seconds on a run-of-the-mill computer. This is a case where threads can be useful to speed things up because many iterations of the same largely mathematical operation are being run.

Let's go ahead and convert this example to a multithreaded program.

With Four Worker Threads

We'll set up four threads that will each run a quarter of the iterations of the loop that generates a random number and tests if it's a Happycoin.

In POSIX C, threads are managed with the pthread_* family of functions. The pthread_create() function is use to create a thread. A function is passed in that will be executed on that thread. Program flow continues on the main thread. The program can wait for a thread's completion by calling pthread_join() on it. You can pass arguments to the function being run on the thread via pthread_create() and get return values from pthread_join().

In our program, we'll isolate the generation of Happycoins in a function called get_happycoins() and that's what will run in our threads. We'll create the four threads, and then immediately wait for the completion of them. Whenever we get the results back from a thread, we'll output them and store the count so we can print the total at the end. To help in passing the results back, we'll create a simple `struct` called `happy_result`.

Make a copy of your existing *happycoin.c* and name it *happycoin-threads.c*. Then in the new file, insert the code in Example 1-10 under the last `#include` in the file.

Example 1-10. ch1-c-threads/happycoin-threads.c

```
#include <pthread.h>

struct happy_result {
  size_t count;
  uint64_t * nums;
};
```

The first line includes `pthread.h`, which gives us access to the various thread functions we'll need. Then `struct happy_result` is defined, which we'll use as the return value for our thread function `get_happycoins()` later on. It stores an array of found happycoins, represented here by a pointer, and the count of them.

Now, go ahead and delete the whole `main()` function because we're about to replace it. First, let's add our `get_happycoins()` function in Example 1-11, which is the code that will run on our worker threads.

Example 1-11. ch1-c-threads/happycoin-threads.c

```
void * get_happycoins(void * arg) {
  int attempts = *(int *)arg;  ❶
  int limit = attempts/10000;
  uint32_t seed = time(NULL);
  uint64_t * nums = malloc(limit * sizeof(uint64_t));
  struct happy_result * result = malloc(sizeof(struct happy_result));
  result->nums = nums;
  result->count = 0;
  for (int i = 1; i < attempts; i++) {
    if (result->count == limit) {
      break;
    }
    uint64_t random_num = random64(&seed);
    if (is_happycoin(random_num)) {
      result->nums[result->count++] = random_num;
    }
  }
  return (void *)result;
}
```

❶ This weird pointer casting thing basically says "treat this arbitrary pointer as a pointer to an `int`, and then get me the value of that `int`."

You'll notice that this function takes in a single void * and returns a single void *. That's the function signature expected by pthread_create(), so we don't have a choice here. This means we have to cast our arguments to what we want them to be. We'll be passing in the number of attempts, so we'll cast the argument to an int. Then, we'll set the seed as we did in the previous example, but this time it's happening in our thread function, so we get a different seed per thread.

After allocating enough space for our array and struct happy_result, we go ahead into the same loop that we did in main() in the single-threaded example, only this time we're putting the results into the struct instead of printing them. Once the loop is done, we return the struct as a pointer, which we cast as void * to satisfy the function signature. This is how information is passed back to the main thread, which will make sense of it.

This demonstrates one of the key properties of threads that we don't get from processes, which is the shared memory space. If, for example, we were using processes instead of threads and some *interprocess communication (IPC)* mechanism to transfer results back, we wouldn't be able to simply pass a memory address back to the main process because the main process wouldn't have access to memory of the worker process. Thanks to virtual memory, the memory address might refer to something else entirely in the main process. Instead of passing a pointer, we'd have to pass the entire value back over the IPC channel, which can introduce performance overhead. Since we're using threads instead of processes, we can just use the pointer, so that the main thread can use it just the same.

Shared memory isn't without its trade-offs, though. In our case, there's no need for the worker thread to make any use of the memory it has now passed to the main thread. This isn't always the case with threads. In a great multitude of cases, it's necessary to properly manage how threads access shared memory via synchronization; otherwise, some unpredictable results may occur. We'll go into how this works in JavaScript in detail in Chapters 4 and 5.

Now, let's wrap this up with the main() function in Example 1-12.

Example 1-12. ch1-c-threads/happycoin-threads.c

```
#define THREAD_COUNT 4

int main() {
  pthread_t thread [THREAD_COUNT];

  int attempts = 10000000/THREAD_COUNT;
  int count = 0;
  for (int i = 0; i < THREAD_COUNT; i++) {
    pthread_create(&thread[i], NULL, get_happycoins, &attempts);
  }
```

```
for (int j = 0; j < THREAD_COUNT; j++) {
  struct happy_result * result;
  pthread_join(thread[j], (void **)&result);
  count += result->count;
  for (int k = 0; k < result->count; k++) {
    printf("%" PRIu64 " ", result->nums[k]);
  }
}
printf("\ncount %d\n", count);
return 0;
}
```

First, we'll declare our four threads as an array on the stack. Then, we divide our desired number of attempts (10,000,000) by the number of threads. This is what will be passed to `get_happycoins()` as an argument, which we see inside the first loop, which creates each of the threads with `pthread_create()`, passing in the number of attempts per thread as an argument. In the next loop, we wait for each of the threads to finish their execution with `pthread_join()`. Then we can print the results and the total from all the threads, just like we would in the single-threaded example.

 This program leaks memory. One hard part of multithreaded programming in C and some other languages is that it can be very easy to lose track of where and when memory is allocated and where and when it should be freed. See if you can modify the code here to ensure the program exits with all heap-allocated memory freed.

With the changes complete, you can compile and run this program with the following commands in your *ch1-c-threads* directory.

```
$ cc -pthread -o happycoin-threads happycoin-threads.c
$ ./happycoin-threads
```

The output should look something like this:

```
24664316829275400000 ... [ 154 more entries ] ... 15764177621931310000
count 156
```

You'll notice output similar to the single-threaded example.[1] You'll also notice that it's a bit faster. On a run-of-the-mill computer it finishes in about 0.8 seconds. This isn't *quite* four times as fast, since there's some initial overhead in the main thread, and also the cost of printing of results. We could print the results as soon as they're ready on the thread that's doing the work, but if we do that, the results may clobber each other in the output because nothing stops two threads from printing to the output

---

1 The fact that the total count from the multithreaded example is different from the single-threaded example is irrelevant because the count is dependent on how many random numbers happened to be Happycoins. The result will be completely different between two different runs.

stream at the same time. By sending the results to the main thread, we can coordinate the printing of results there so that nothing gets clobbered.

This illustrates the primary advantage and one drawback of threaded code. On one hand, it's useful for splitting up computationally expensive tasks so that they can be run in parallel. On the other hand, we need to ensure that some events are properly synchronized so that weird errors don't occur. When adding threads to your code in any language, it's worth making sure that the use is appropriate. Also, as with any exercise in attempting to make faster programs, always be measuring. You don't want to have the complexity of threaded code in your application if it doesn't turn out to give you any actual benefit.

Any programming language supporting threads is going to provide some mechanisms for creating and destroying threads, passing messages in between, and interacting with data that's shared between the threads. This may not look the same in every language, because as languages and their paradigms are different, so are their programmatic models of parallel programming. Now that we've explored what threaded programs look like in a low-level language like C, let's dive in to JavaScript. Things will look a little different, but as you'll see, the principles remain the same.

Browsers

JavaScript doesn't have a single, bespoke implementation like most other programming languages do. For example, with Python, you're probably going to run the Python binary provided by the language maintainers. JavaScript, on the other hand, has many different implementations. This includes the JavaScript engine that ships with different web browsers, such as V8 in Chrome, SpiderMonkey in Firefox, and JavaScriptCore in Safari. The V8 engine is also used by Node.js on the server.

These separate implementations each start off by implementing some facsimile of the ECMAScript specification. As the compatibility charts that we so often need to consult suggest, not every engine implements JavaScript the same way. Certainly, browser vendors attempt to implement JavaScript features in the same manner, but bugs do happen. At the language level, there are some concurrency primitives that have been made available, which are covered in more detail in Chapters 4 and 5.

Other APIs are also added in each implementation to make the JavaScript that can be run even more powerful. This chapter focuses entirely on the multithreaded APIs that are provided by modern web browsers, the most approachable of which is the web worker.

Using these worker threads is beneficial for many reasons, but one that is particularly applicable to browsers is that, by offloading CPU-intensive work to a separate thread, the main thread is then able to dedicate more resources to rendering the UI. This can help contribute to a smoother, more user-friendly experience than what might have been traditionally achievable.

Dedicated Workers

Web workers allow you to spawn a new environment for executing JavaScript in. JavaScript that is executed in this way is allowed to run in a separate thread from the JavaScript that spawned it. Communication occurs between these two environments by using a pattern called *message passing*. Recall that it's JavaScript's nature to be single-threaded. Web workers play nicely with this nature and expose message passing by way of triggering functions to be run by the event loop.

It's possible for a JavaScript environment to spawn more than one web worker, and a given web worker is free to spawn even more web workers. That said, if you find yourself spawning massive hierarchies of web workers, you might need to reevaluate your application.

There is more than one type of web worker, the simplest of which is the dedicated worker.

Dedicated Worker Hello World

The best way to learn a new technology is to actually work with it. The relationship between page and worker that you are building is displayed in Figure 2-1. In this case you'll create just a single worker, but a hierarchy of workers is also achievable.

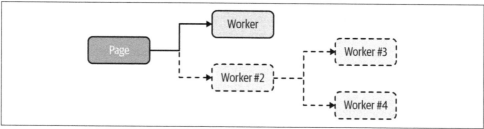

Figure 2-1. Dedicated worker relationship

First, create a directory named *ch2-web-workers/*. You'll keep the three example files required for this project in there. Next, create an *index.html* file inside the directory. JavaScript that runs in the browser needs to first be loaded by a web page, and this file represents the basis of that web page. Add the content from Example 2-1 to this file to kick things off.

Example 2-1. ch2-web-workers/index.html

```html
<html>
  <head>
    <title>Web Workers Hello World</title>
    <script src="main.js"></script>
  </head>
</html>
```

As you can see, this file is super basic. All it is doing is setting a title and loading a single JavaScript file named *main.js*. The remaining sections in this chapter follow a similar pattern. The more interesting part is what's inside the *main.js* file.

In fact, create that *main.js* file now, and add the content from Example 2-2 to it.

Example 2-2. ch2-web-workers/main.js

```javascript
console.log('hello from main.js');

const worker = new Worker('worker.js'); ❶

worker.onmessage = (msg) => { ❷
  console.log('message received from worker', msg.data);
};

worker.postMessage('message sent to worker'); ❸

console.log('hello from end of main.js');
```

❶ Instantiation of a new dedicated worker.

❷ A message handler is attached to the worker.

❸ A message is passed into the worker.

The first thing that happens in this file is that a call to `console.log()` is made. This is to make it obvious the order in which files get executed. The next thing that happens is that a new dedicated worker gets instantiated. This is done by calling `new Worker(filename)`. Once called, the JavaScript engine begins the download (or cache lookup) for the appropriate file in the background.

Next, a handler for the `message` event is attached to the worker. This is done by assigning a function to the `.onmessage` property of the dedicated worker. When a message is received, that function gets called. The argument provided to the function is an instance of `MessageEvent`. It comes with a bunch of properties, but the one that's most interesting is the `.data` property. This represents the object that was returned from the dedicated worker.

Finally, a call to the dedicated worker's `.postMessage()` method is made. This is how the JavaScript environment that instantiates the dedicated worker is able to communicate with the dedicated worker. In this case a basic string has been passed into the dedicated worker. There are restrictions on what kind of data can be passed into this method; see the Appendix, *Structured Clone Algorithm* for more details.

Now that your main JavaScript file is finished, you're ready to create the file that will be executed within the dedicated worker. Create a new file named *worker.js* and add the contents of Example 2-3 to it.

Example 2-3. ch2-web-workers/worker.js

```
console.log('hello from worker.js');

self.onmessage = (msg) => {
  console.log('message from main', msg.data);

  postMessage('message sent from worker');
};
```

In this file a single global function named `onmessage` is defined and a function is assigned to it. This `onmessage` function, inside the dedicated worker, is called when the `worker.postMessage()` method is called from outside the dedicated worker. This assignment could also have been written as `onmessage =` or even `var onmessage =`, but using `const onmessage =` or `let onmessage =` or even declaring `function onmessage` won't work. The `self` identifier is an alias for `globalThis` inside a web worker where the otherwise familiar `window` isn't available.

Inside the `onmessage` function, the code first prints the message that was received from outside of the dedicated worker. After that, it calls the `postMessage()` global function. This method takes an argument, and the argument is then provided to the calling environment by triggering the dedicated worker's `onmessage()` method. The same rules about message passing and object cloning also apply here. Again, the example is just using a simple string for now.

There are some additional rules when it comes to loading a dedicated worker script file. The file that is loaded must be in the same origin that the main JavaScript environment is running in. Also, browsers won't allow you to run dedicated workers when JavaScript runs using the `file://` protocol, which is a fancy way of saying you can't simply double-click the *index.html* file and view the application running. Instead, you'll need to run your application from a web server. Luckily, if you have a recent Node.js installed, you can run the following command to start a very basic web server locally:

```
$ npx serve .
```

Once executed, this command spins up a server that hosts files from the local filesystem. It also displays the URL that the server is available as. Typically the command outputs the following URL, assuming the port is free:

```
http://localhost:5000
```

Copy whatever URL was provided to you and open it using a web browser. When the page first opens you'll most likely see a plain, white screen. But that's not a problem because all of the output is being displayed in the web developer console. Different browsers make the console available in different ways, but usually you can right-click somewhere in the background and click the Inspect menu option, or you can press Ctrl+Shift+I (or Cmd-Shift-I) to open up the inspector. Once in the inspector, click on the Console tab, and then refresh the page just in case any console messages weren't captured. Once that's done you should see the messages that are displayed in Table 2-1.

Table 2-1. Example console output

Log	Location
hello from main.js	main.js:1:9
hello from end of main.js	main.js:11:9
hello from worker.js	worker.js:1:9
message from main, message sent to worker	worker.js:4:11
message received from worker, message sent from worker	main.js:6:11

This output confirms the order in which the messages have been executed, though it's not entirely deterministic. First, the *main.js* file is loaded, and its output is printed. The worker is instantiated and configured, its `postMessage()` method is called, and then the last message gets printed as well. Next, the *worker.js* file is run, and its message handler is called, printing a message. It then calls `postMessage()` to send a message back to *main.js*. Finally, the `onmessage` handler for the dedicated worker is called in *main.js*, and the final message is printed.

Advanced Dedicated Worker Usage

Now that you're familiar with the basics of dedicated workers, you're ready to work with some of the more complex features.

When you work with JavaScript that doesn't involve dedicated workers, all the code you end up loading is available in the same realm. Loading new JavaScript code is done either by loading a script with a `<script>` tag, or by making an XHR request and using the eval() function with a string representing the code. When it comes to dedicated workers, you can't inject a <script> tag into the DOM because there's no DOM associated with the worker.

Instead, you can make use of the importScripts() function, which is a global function only available within web workers. This function accepts one or more arguments that represent the paths to scripts to be loaded. These scripts will be loaded from the same origin as the web page. These scripts are loaded in a synchronous manner, so code that follows the function call will run after the scripts are loaded.

Instances of Worker inherit from EventTarget and have some generic methods for dealing with events. However, the Worker class provides the most important methods on the instance. The following is a list of these methods, some of which you've already worked with, some of which are new:

worker.postMessage(msg)
> This sends a message to the worker that is handled by the event loop before invoking the self.onmessage function, passing in msg.

worker.onmessage
> If assigned, it is in turn invoked when the self.postMessage function inside the worker is called.

worker.onerror
> If assigned, it is invoked when an error is thrown inside the worker. A single ErrorEvent argument is provided, having .colno, .lineno, .filename, and .message properties. This error will bubble up unless you call err.preventDefault().

worker.onmessageerror
> If assigned, this is invoked when the worker receives a message that it cannot deserialize.

worker.terminate()
> If called, the worker terminates immediately. Future calls to worker.postMessage() will silently fail.

Inside the dedicated worker, the global self variable is an instance of WorkerGlobalScope. The most notable addition is the importScripts() function for injecting new JavaScript files. Some of the high-level communication APIs like XMLHttpRequest, WebSocket, and fetch() are available. Useful functions that aren't necessarily part of JavaScript but are rebuilt by every major engine, like setTimeout(), setInterval(), atob(), and btoa(), are also available. The two data-storage APIs, localStorage and indexedDB, are available.

When it comes to APIs that are missing, though, you'll need to experiment and see what you have access to. Generally, APIs that modify the global state of the web page aren't available. In the main JavaScript realm, the global `location` is available and is an instance of `Location`. Inside a dedicated worker, `location` is still available, but it's an instance of `WorkerLocation` and is a little different, notably missing a `.reload()` method that can cause a page refresh. The `document` global is also missing, which is the API for accessing the page's DOM.

When instantiating a dedicated worker, there is an optional second argument for specifying the options for the worker. The instantiation takes on the following signature:

```
const worker = new Worker(filename, options);
```

The `options` argument is an object that can contain the properties listed here:

type
: Either `classic` (default), for a classic JavaScript file, or `module`, to specify an ECMAScript Module (ESM).

credentials
: This value determines if HTTP credentials are sent with the request to get the worker file. The value can be `omit` to exclude the credentials, `same-origin` to send credentials (but only if the origin matches), or `include` to always send the credentials.

name
: This names a dedicated worker and is mostly used for debugging. The value is provided in the worker as a global named `name`.

Shared Workers

A *shared worker* is another type of web worker, but what makes it special is that a shared worker can be accessed by different browser environments, such as different windows (tabs), across iframes, and even from different web workers. They also have a different `self` within the worker, being an instance of `SharedWorkerGlobalScope`. A shared worker can only be accessed by JavaScript running on the same origin. For example, a window running on *http://localhost:5000* cannot access a shared worker running on *http://google.com:80*.

Shared workers are currently disabled in Safari (*https://oreil.ly/eHlkL*), and this seems to have been true since at least 2013, which will undoubtedly harm adoption of the technology.

Before diving into code, it's important to consider a few gotchas. One thing that makes shared workers a little hard to reason about is that they aren't necessarily attached to a particular window (environment). Sure, they're initially spawned by a particular window, but after that they can end up "belonging" to multiple windows. That means that when the first window is closed, the shared worker is kept around.

 Since shared workers don't belong to a particular window, one interesting question is where should `console.log` output go? As of Firefox v85, the output is associated with the first window that spawns the shared worker. Open another window and the first still gets the logs. Close the first window and the logs are now invisible. Open another window and the historical logs then appear in the newest window. Chrome v87, on the other hand, doesn't display shared worker logs at all. Keep this in mind when debugging.

Debugging Shared Workers

Both Firefox and Chrome offer a dedicated way to debug shared workers. In Firefox, visit *about:debugging* in the address bar. Next, click This Firefox in the left column. Then, scroll down until you see the Shared Workers section with a list of shared worker scripts. In our case we see an Inspect button next to an entry for the *shared-worker.js* file. With Chrome, visit *chrome://inspect/#workers*, find the *shared-worker.js* entry, and then click the "inspect" link next to it. With both browsers you'll be taken to a dedicated console attached to the worker.

Shared workers can be used to hold a semipersistent state that is maintained when other windows connect to it. For example, if Window 1 tells the shared worker to write a value, then Window 2 can ask the shared worker to read that value back. Refresh Window 1 and the value is still maintained. Refresh Window 2 and it's also retained. Close Window 1 and it's still retained. However, once you close or refresh the final window that is still using the shared worker, the state will be lost and the shared worker script will be evaluated again.

 A shared worker JavaScript file is cached while multiple windows are using it; refreshing a page won't necessarily reload your changes. Instead, you'll need to close other open browser windows, then refresh the remaining window, to get the browser to run your new code.

With these caveats in mind, you're now ready to build a simple application that uses shared workers.

Shared Worker Hello World

A shared worker is "keyed" based on its location in the current origin. For example, the shared worker you'll work with in this example is located somewhere like *http://localhost:5000/shared-worker.js*. Whether the worker is loaded from an HTML file located at */red.html*, */blue.html*, or even */foo/index.html*, the shared worker instance will always remain the same. There is a way to create different shared worker instances using the same JavaScript file, and that's covered in "Advanced Shared Worker Usage" on page 32.

The relationship between the page and the worker that you are building is displayed in Figure 2-2.

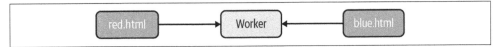

Figure 2-2. Shared worker relationship

Now, it's time to create some files. For this example, create a directory named *ch2-shared-workers/*, and all the files necessary will live in this directory. Once that's done, create an HTML file containing the content in Example 2-4.

Example 2-4. ch2-shared-workers/red.html

```
<html>
  <head>
    <title>Shared Workers Red</title>
    <script src="red.js"></script>
  </head>
</html>
```

Much like the HTML file you created in the previous section, this one just sets a title and loads a JavaScript file. Once that's done, create another HTML file containing the content in Example 2-5.

Example 2-5. ch2-shared-workers/blue.html

```
<html>
  <head>
    <title>Shared Workers Blue</title>
    <script src="blue.js"></script>
  </head>
</html>
```

For this example you're going to work with two separate HTML files, each representing a new JavaScript environment that will be available on the same origin. Technically, you could have reused the same HTML file in both windows, but we want to make it very explicit that none of the state is going to be associated with the HTML files or the *red/blue* JavaScript files.

Next, you're ready to create the first JavaScript file loaded directly by an HTML file. Create a file containing the content in Example 2-6.

Example 2-6. ch2-shared-workers/red.js

```
console.log('red.js');

const worker = new SharedWorker('shared-worker.js'); ❶

worker.port.onmessage = (event) => { ❷
  console.log('EVENT', event.data);
};
```

❶ Instantiate the shared worker

❷ Note the worker.port property for communications

This JavaScript file is rather basic. What it does is instantiate a shared worker instance by calling new SharedWorker(). After that it adds a handler for message events that are emitted from the shared worker. When a message is received, it is simply printed to the console.

Unlike with Worker instances, where you called .onmessage directly, with SharedWorker instances you'll make use of the .port property.

Next, copy and paste the *red.js* file that you created in Example 2-6 and name it *blue.js*. Update the console.log() call to print *blue.js*; otherwise, the content will remain the same.

Finally, create a *shared-worker.js* file, containing the content in Example 2-7. This is where most of the magic will happen.

Example 2-7. ch2-shared-workers/shared-worker.js

```
const ID = Math.floor(Math.random() * 999999); ❶
console.log('shared-worker.js', ID);

const ports = new Set(); ❷

self.onconnect = (event) => { ❸
  const port = event.ports[0];
  ports.add(port);
  console.log('CONN', ID, ports.size);

  port.onmessage = (event) => { ❹
```

```
    console.log('MESSAGE', ID, event.data);

    for (let p of ports) { ❺
      p.postMessage([ID, event.data]);
    }
  };
};
```

❶ Random ID for debugging

❷ Singleton list of ports

❸ Connection event handler

❹ Callback when a new message is received

❺ Messages are dispatched to each window

The first thing that happens in this file is that a random ID value is generated. This value is printed in the console and later passed to the calling JavaScript environments. It's not particularly useful with a real application, but it does a great job proving that state is retained, and when state is lost, when dealing with this shared worker.

Next, a singleton `Set` named `ports` is created.[1] This will contain a list of all of the ports that are made available to the worker. Both the `worker.port` available in the window and the `port` provided in a service worker are an instance of the `Message Port` class.

The final thing that happens in the outer scope of this shared worker file is that a listener for the `connect` event is established. This function is called every time a JavaScript environment creates a `SharedWorker` instance that references this shared worker. When this listener is called, an instance of `MessageEvent` is provided as the argument.

There are several properties available on the `connect` event, but the most important one is the `ports` property. This property is an array that contains a single element which is a reference to the `MessagePort` instance that allows communication with the calling JavaScript environment. This particular port is then added to the `ports` set.

An event listener for the `message` event is also attached to the port. Much like the `onmessage` method you used previously with the `Worker` instance, this method is called when one of the external JavaScript environments calls the

---

1 As of Firefox v85, regardless of how many entries are in the `ports` set, calling `console.log(ports)` will always display a single entry. For now, to debug the size, call `console.log(ports.size)` instead.

applicable `.postMessage()` method. When a message is received, the code prints the ID value and the data that was received.

The event listener also dispatches the message back to the calling environments. It does this by iterating the `ports` set, calling the `.postMessage()` method for each of the encountered ports. Since this method only takes a single argument, an array is passed in to sort of emulate multiple arguments. The first element of this array is the ID value again, and the second is the data that was passed in.

If you've worked with WebSockets using Node.js before, then this code pattern might feel familiar. With most popular WebSockets packages, an event is triggered when a connection is made, and the connection argument can then have a message listener attached to it.

At this point you're ready to test your application again. First, run the following command inside your *ch2-shared-workers/* directory, and then copy and paste the URL that is displayed:

```
$ npx serve .
```

Again, in our case, we're given the URL *http://localhost:5000*. This time, though, instead of opening the URL directly, you'll want to first open the web inspector in your browser and then open a modified version of the URL.

Switch to your browser and open a new tab. It's fine if this opens your home page, a blank tab, or whatever your default page is. Then, open the web inspector again and navigate to the console tab. Once that's done, paste the URL that was given to you, but modify it to open the */red.html* page. The URL that you enter might look something like this:

```
http://localhost:5000/red.html
```

Press Enter to open the page. The `serve` package will probably redirect your browser from */red.html* to */red*, but that's fine.

Once the page has loaded, you should see the messages listed in Table 2-2 displayed in your console. If you open the inspector after loading the page, then you probably won't see any logs, though doing so then refreshing the page should display the logs. Note that at the time of writing, only Firefox will display messages generated in *shared-worker.js*.

Table 2-2. First window console output

Log	Location
red.js	red.js:1:9
shared-worker.js 278794	shared-worker.js:2:9
CONN 278794 1	shared-worker.js:9:11

In our case we can see that the *red.js* file was executed, that this particular *shared-worker.js* instance generated an ID of 278794, and that there is currently a single window connected to this shared worker.

Next, open another browser window. Again, open the web inspector first, switch to the Console tab, paste the base URL that was provided by the `serve` command, and then add */blue.html* to the end of the URL. In our case the URL looks like this:

```
http://localhost:5000/blue.html
```

Press Enter to open the URL. Once the page loads, you should only see a single message printed in the console output stating that the *blue.js* file was executed. At this point it's not too interesting. But switch back to the previous window you had opened for the *red.html* page. You should see that the new log listed in Table 2-3 has been added.

Table 2-3. First window console output, continued

Log	Location
CONN 278794 2	shared-worker.js:9:11

Now things are getting a little exciting. The shared worker environment now has two references to a `MessagePort` instance pointing to two separate windows. At the same time, two windows have references to `MessagePort` instances for the same shared worker.

Now you're ready to send a message to the shared worker from one of the windows. Switch focus to the console window and type in the following command:

```
worker.port.postMessage('hello, world');
```

Press Enter to execute that line of JavaScript. You should see a message in the first console that is generated in the shared worker, a message in the first console from *red.js*, and a message in the second window's console from *blue.js*. In our case we see the outputs listed in Table 2-4.

Table 2-4. First and second window console output

Log	Location	Console
MESSAGE 278794 hello, world	shared-worker.js:12:13	1
EVENT Array [278794, "hello, world"]	red.js:6:11	1
EVENT Array [278794, "hello, world"]	blue.js:6:11	2

At this point you've successfully sent a message from the JavaScript environment available in one window to the JavaScript environment in a shared worker, and then passed a message from the worker to two separate windows.

Advanced Shared Worker Usage

Shared workers are governed by the same object cloning rules described in the Appendix. Also, like their dedicated worker equivalent, shared workers also have access to the `importScripts()` function for loading external JavaScript files. As of Firefox v85/Chrome v87 you may find Firefox more convenient to debug shared workers with due to the output of `console.log()` from the shared worker being available.

The shared worker instances do have access to a `connect` event, which can be handled with the `self.onconnect()` method. Notably missing, especially if you're familiar with WebSockets, is a `disconnect` or `close` event.

When it comes to creating a singleton collection of `port` instances, like in the sample code in this section, it's very easy to create a memory leak. In this case, just keep refreshing one of the windows, and each refresh adds a new entry to the set.

This is far from ideal. One thing you can do to address this is to add an event listener in your main JavaScript environments (i.e., *red.js* and *blue.js*) that fires when the page is being torn down. Have this event listener pass a special message to the shared worker. Within the shared worker, when the message is received, remove the port from the list of ports. Here's an example of how to do this:

```
// main JavaScript file
window.addEventListener('beforeunload', () => {
  worker.port.postMessage('close');
});

// shared worker
port.onmessage = (event) => {
  if (event.data === 'close') {
    ports.delete(port);
    return;
  }
};
```

Unfortunately, there are still situations where a port can stick around. If the `beforeun load` event doesn't fire, or if an error happens when it's fired, or if the page crashes in an unanticipated way, this can lead to expired port references sticking around in the shared worker.

A more robust system would also need a way for the shared worker to occasionally "ping" the calling environments, sending a special message via `port.postMessage()`, and have the calling environments reply. With such an approach the shared worker can delete port instances if it doesn't receive a reply within a certain amount of time. But even this approach isn't perfect, as a slow JavaScript environment can lead to long response times. Luckily, interacting with ports that no longer have a valid JavaScript associated with them doesn't have much of a side effect.

The full constructor for the `SharedWorker` class looks like this:

```
const worker = new SharedWorker(filename, nameOrOptions);
```

The signature is slightly different than when instantiating a `Worker` instance, notably that the second argument can either be an options object, or the name of the worker. Much like with a `Worker` instance, the name of the worker is available inside the worker as `self.name`.

At this point you may be wondering how that works. For example, could the shared worker be declared in *red.js* with a name of "red worker" and in *blue.js* with a name of "blue worker"? In this case, two *separate* workers will be created, each with a different global environment, a different ID value, and the appropriate `self.name`.

You can think of these shared worker instances as being "keyed" by not only their URL but also their name. This may be why the signature changes between a `Worker` and a `SharedWorker`, as the name is much more important for the latter.

Other than the ability to replace the options argument with a string name, the options argument for a `SharedWorker` is exactly the same as it is for a `Worker`.

In this example, you've only created a single `SharedWorker` instance per window, assigned to `worker`, but there is nothing stopping you from creating multiple instances. In fact, you can even create multiple shared workers that point to the same instance, assuming the URLs and names match. When this happens, both of the `SharedWorker` instances' `.port` properties are able to receive messages.

These `SharedWorker` instances are definitely capable of maintaining state between page loads. You've been doing just that, with the `ID` variable holding a unique number and `ports` containing a list of ports. This state even persists through refreshes as long as one window remains open, like if you were to refresh the *blue.html* page followed by the *red.html* page. However, that state would be lost if both pages were refreshed simultaneously, one closed and the other refreshed, or if both were closed. In the next section you'll work with a technology that can continue to maintain state—and run code—even when connected windows are closed.

Service Workers

A *service worker* functions as a sort of proxy that sits between one or more web pages running in the browser and the server. Because a service worker isn't associated with just a single web page but potentially multiple pages, it's more similar to a shared worker than to a dedicated worker. They're even "keyed" in the same manner as shared workers. But a service worker can exist and run in the background even when a page isn't necessarily still open. Because of this you can think of a dedicated worker as being associated with one page, a shared worker as being associated with one or more pages, but a service worker as being associated with zero or more pages. But a shared worker doesn't magically spawn into existence. Instead, it does require a web page to be opened first to install the shared worker.

Service workers are primarily intended for performing cache management of a website or a single page application. They are most commonly invoked when network requests are sent to the server, wherein an event handler inside the service worker intercepts the network request. The service worker's claim to fame is that it can be used to return cached assets when a browser displays a web page but the computer it's running on no longer has network access. When the service worker receives the request, it may consult a cache to find a cached resource, make a request to the server to retrieve some semblance of the resource, or even perform a heavy computation and return the result. While this last option makes it similar to the other web workers you've looked at, you really shouldn't use service workers just for the purpose of offloading CPU-intensive work to another thread.

Service workers expose a larger API than that of the other web workers, though their primary use case is not for offloading heavy computation from the main thread. Service workers are certainly complex enough to have entire books dedicated to them. That said, because the primary goal of this book is to teach you about the multithreaded capabilities of JavaScript, we won't cover them in their entirety. For example, there's an entire Push API available for receiving messages pushed to the browser from the server that won't be covered at all.

Much like with the other web workers, a service worker can't access the DOM. They also can't make blocking requests. For example, setting the third argument of XMLHttpRequest#open() to false, which would block code execution until the request succeeds or times out, is not allowed. Browsers will only allow service workers to run on a web page that has been served using the HTTPS protocol. Luckily for us, there is one notable exception, where localhost may load service workers using HTTP. This is to make local development easier. Firefox doesn't allow service workers when using its Private Browsing feature. Chrome, however, does allow service workers when using its Incognito feature. That said, a service worker instance can't communicate between a normal and Incognito window.

Both Firefox and Chrome have an Applications panel in the inspector that contains a Service Workers section. You can use this to both view any service workers associated with the current page and to also perform a very important development action: unregister them, which basically allows you to reset the browser state to before the worker was registered. Unfortunately, as of the current browser versions, these browser panels don't provide a way to hop into the JavaScript inspectors for the service workers.

Now that you're aware of some of the gotchas with service workers, you're ready to build one out.

Service Worker Hello World

In this section you're going to build a very basic service worker that intercepts all HTTP requests sent from a basic web page. Most of the requests will pass through to the server unaltered. However, requests made to a specific resource will instead return a value that is calculated by the service worker itself. Most service workers would instead do a lot of cache lookups, but again, the goal is to show off service workers from a multithreaded point of view.

The first file you'll need is again an HTML file. Make a new directory named *ch2-service-workers/*. Then, inside this directory, create a file with the content from Example 2-8.

Example 2-8. ch2-service-workers/index.html

```
<html>
  <head>
    <title>Service Workers Example</title>
    <script src="main.js"></script>
  </head>
</html>
```

This is a rather basic file that just loads your application's JavaScript file, which comes next. Create a file named *main.js*, and add the content from Example 2-9 to it.

Example 2-9. ch2-service-workers/main.js

```
navigator.serviceWorker.register('/sw.js', { ❶
  scope: '/'
});
```

```
navigator.serviceWorker.oncontrollerchange = () => { ❷
  console.log('controller change');
};

async function makeRequest() { ❸
  const result = await fetch('/data.json');
  const payload = await result.json();
  console.log(payload);
}
```

❶ Registers service worker and defines scope.

❷ Listens for a `controllerchange` event.

❸ Function to initiate request.

Now things are starting to get a little interesting. The first thing going on in this file is that the service worker is created. Unlike the other web workers you worked with, you aren't using the `new` keyword with a constructor. Instead, this code depends on the `navigator.serviceWorker` object to create the worker. The first argument is the path to the JavaScript file that acts as the service worker. The second argument is an optional configuration object that supports a single `scope` property.

The `scope` represents the directory for the current origin wherein any HTML pages that are loaded in it will have their requests passed through the service worker. By default, the `scope` value is the same as the directory that the service worker is loaded from. In this case, the / value is relative to the *index.html* directory, and because *sw.js* is located in the same directory, we could have omitted the scope and it would behave exactly the same.

Once the service worker has been installed for the page, all outbound HTTP requests will get sent through the service worker. This includes requests made to different origins. Since the scope for this page is set to the uppermost directory of the origin, any HTML page that is opened in this origin will then have to make requests through the service worker for assets. If the `scope` had been set to */foo*, then a page opened at */bar.html* will be unaffected by the service worker, but a page at */foo/baz.html* would be affected.

The next thing that happens is that a listener for the `controllerchange` event is added to the `navigator.serviceWorker` object. When this listener fires, a message is printed to the console. This message is just for debugging when a service worker takes control of a page that has been loaded and which is within the scope of the worker.

Finally, a function named `makeRequest()` is defined. This function makes a GET request to the */data.json* path, decodes the response as JavaScript Object Notation

---

(JSON), and prints the result. As you might have noticed, there aren't any references to that function. Instead, you'll manually run it in the console later to test the functionality.

With that file out of the way, you're now ready to create the service worker itself. Create a third file named *sw.js*, and add the content from Example 2-10 to it.

Example 2-10. ch2-service-workers/sw.js

```
let counter = 0;

self.oninstall = (event) => {
  console.log('service worker install');
};

self.onactivate = (event) => {
  console.log('service worker activate');
  event.waitUntil(self.clients.claim()); ❶
};

self.onfetch = (event) => {
  console.log('fetch', event.request.url);

  if (event.request.url.endsWith('/data.json')) {
    counter++;
    event.respondWith( ❷
      new Response(JSON.stringify({counter}), {
        headers: {
          'Content-Type': 'application/json'
        }
      })
    );
    return;
  }

  // fallback to normal HTTP request
  event.respondWith(fetch(event.request)); ❸
};
```

❶ Allows service worker to claim the opened *index.html* page.

❷ Override for when */data.json* is requested.

❸ Other URLs will fall back to a normal network request.

The first thing that happens in this file is that a global variable counter is initialized to zero. Later, when certain types of requests are intercepted, that number will increment. This is just an example to prove that the service worker is running; in a real application you should never store state that's meant to be persistent in this way. In fact, expect any service workers to start and stop fairly frequently, in a manner that's hard to predict and that differs depending on browser implementation.

After that, we create a handler for the `install` event by assigning a function to `self.oninstall`. This function runs when this version of the service worker is installed for the very first time in the browser. Most real-world applications will perform instantiation work at this stage. For example, there's an object available at `self.caches` which can be used to configure caches that store the result of network requests. However, because this basic application doesn't have much to do in the way of instantiation, it just prints a message and finishes.

Next up is a function for handling the `activate` event. This event is useful for performing cleanup work when new versions of the service worker are introduced. With a real-world application, it's probably going to do work like tearing down old versions of caches.

In this case, the `activate` handler function is making a call to the `self.cli ents.claim()` method. Calling this allows the page instance that first created the service worker, that is, the *index.html* page you'll open for the first time, to then get controlled by the service worker. If you didn't have this line, the page wouldn't be controlled by the service worker when first loaded. However, refreshing the page or opening *index.html* in another tab would then allow that page to be controlled.

The call to `self.clients.claim()` returns a promise. Sadly, event handler functions used in service workers are not async functions able to `await` promises. However, the `event` argument is an object with a `.waitUntil()` method, which does work with a promise. Once the promise provided to that method resolves, it will allow the `oninstall` and `onactivate` (and later `onfetch`) handlers to finish. By not calling that method, like in the `oninstall` handler, the step is considered finished once the function exits.

The last event handler is the `onfetch` function. This one is the most complex and also the one that will be called the most throughout the lifetime of the service worker. This handler is called every time a network request is made by a web page under control of the service worker. It's called `onfetch` to signal that it correlates to the `fetch()` function in the browser, though it's almost a misnomer because any network request will be passed through it. For example, if an image tag is later added to the page, the request would also trigger `onfetch`.

This function first logs a message to confirm that it's being run and also printing the URL that is being requested. Other information about the requested resource is also available, such as headers and the HTTP method. In a real-world application this information can be used to consult with a cache to see if the resource already exists. For example, a `GET` request to a resource within the current origin could be served from the cache, but if it doesn't exist, it could be requested using the fetch() function, then inserted into the cache, then returned to the browser.

This basic example just takes the URL and checks to see if it's for a URL that ends in */data.json*. If it is not, the if statement body is skipped, and the final line of the function is called. This line just takes the request object (which is an instance of Request), passes it to the fetch() method, which returns a promise, and passes that promise to event.respondWith(). The fetch() method will resolve an object that will then be used to represent the response, which is then provided to the browser. This is essentially a very basic HTTP proxy.

However, circling back to the */data.json* URL check, if it does pass, then something more complicated happens. In that case the counter variable is incremented, and a new response is generated from scratch (which is an instance of Response). In this case, a JSON string is constructed that contains the counter value. This is provided as the first argument to Response, which represents the response body. The second argument contains meta information about the response. In this case the Content-Type header is set to application/json, which suggests to the browser that the response is a JSON payload.

Now that your files have been created, navigate to the directory where you created them using your console and run the following command to start another web server:

```
$ npx serve .
```

Again, copy the URL that was provided, open a new web browser window, open the inspector, then paste the URL to visit the page. You should see this message printed in your console (and possibly others):

```
controller change               main.js:6:11
```

Next, browse to the list of service workers installed in your browser using the aforementioned technique. Within the inspector, you should see the previously logged messages; specifically you should see these two:

```
service worker install        sw.js:4:11
service worker activate        sw.js:8:11
```

Next, switch back to the browser window. While in the Console tab of the inspector, run the following line of code:

```
makeRequest();
```

This runs the makeRequest() function, which triggers an HTTP GET request to */data.json* of the current origin. Once it completes, you should see the message Object { counter: 1 } displayed in your console. That message was generated using the service worker, and the request was never sent to the web server. If you switch to the network tab of the inspector, you should see what looks like an otherwise normal request to get the resource. If you click the request, you should see that it replied with a 200 status code, and the `Content-Type` header should be set to `application/json` as well. As far as the web page is concerned, it did make a normal HTTP request. But you know better.

Switch back to the service worker inspector console. In here, you should see that a third message has been printed containing the details of the request. On our machine we get the following:

```
fetch http://localhost:5000/data.json    sw.js:13:11
```

At this point you've successfully intercepted an HTTP request from one JavaScript environment, performed some computation in another environment, and returned the result back to the main environment. Much like with the other web workers, this calculation was done in a separate thread, running code in parallel. Had the service worker done some very heavy and slow calculations, the web page would have been free to perform other actions while it waited for the response.

 In your first browser window, you might have noticed an error that an attempt to download the *favicon.ico* file was made but failed. You might also be wondering why the shared worker console doesn't mention this file. That's because, at the point when the window was first opened, it wasn't yet under control of the service worker, so the request was made directly over the network, bypassing the worker. Debugging service workers can be confusing, and this is one of the caveats to keep in mind.

Now that you've built a working service worker, you're ready to learn about some of the more advanced features they have to offer.

Advanced Service Worker Concepts

Service workers are intended to only be used for performing asynchronous operations. Because of that, the `localStorage` API, which technically blocks when reading and writing, isn't available. However, the asynchronous `indexedDB` API is available. Top-level `await` is disabled within service workers as well.

When it comes to keeping track of state, you'll mostly be using `self.caches` and `indexedDB`. Again, keeping data in a global variable isn't going to be reliable. In fact, while debugging your service workers, you might find that they occasionally end up stopped, at which point you're not allowed to hop into the inspector. The browsers have a button that allows you to start the worker again, allowing you to hop back into the inspector. It's this stopping and starting that flushes out global state.

Service worker scripts are cached rather aggressively by the browser. When reloading the page, the browser may make a request for the script, but unless the script has changed, it won't be considered for being replaced. The Chrome browser does offer the ability to trigger an update to the script when reloading the page; to do this, navigate to the Application tab in the inspector, then click "Service Workers," then click the "Update on reload" checkbox.

Every service worker goes through a state change from the time of its inception until the time it can be used. This state is available within the service worker by reading the `self.serviceWorker.state` property. Here's a list of the stages it goes through:

parsed
> This is the very first state of the service worker. At this point the JavaScript content of the file has been parsed. This is more of an internal state that you'll probably never encounter in your application.

installing
> The installation has begun but is not yet complete. This happens once per worker version. This state is active after `oninstall` is called and before the `event.respondWith()` promise has resolved.

installed
> At this point the installation is complete. The `onactivate` handler is going to be called next. In my testing I find that the service workers jump from `installing` to `activating` so fast that I never see the `installed` state.

activating
> This state happens when `onactivate` is called but the `event.respondWith()` promise hasn't yet resolved.

activated
> The activation is complete, and the worker is ready to do its thing. At this point `fetch` events will get intercepted.

redundant
> At this point, a newer version of the script has been loaded, and the previous script is no longer necessary. This can also be triggered if the worker script download fails, if it contains a syntax error, or if an error is thrown.

Philosophically, service workers should be treated as a form of progressive enhancement. This means that any web pages using them should still behave as usual if the service worker isn't used at all. This is important because you might encounter a browser that doesn't support service workers, or the installation phase might fail, or privacy-conscientious users might disable them entirely. In other words, if you're only looking to add multithreading capabilities to your application, then choose one of the other web workers instead.

The global `self` object used inside service workers is an instance of `ServiceWorker GlobalScope`. The `importScripts()` function available in other web workers is available in this environment as well. Like the other workers, it's also possible to pass messages into, and receive messages from, a service worker. The same `self.onmessage` handler can be assigned. This can, perhaps, be used to signal to the service worker that it should perform some sort of cache invalidation. Again, messages passed in this way are subject to the same cloning algorithm that we discuss in the Appendix.

While debugging your service workers, and the requests that are being made from your browser, you'll need to keep caching in mind. Not only can the service worker implement caches that you control programmatically, but the browser itself also still has to deal with regular network caching. This can mean requests sent from your service worker to the server might not always be received by the server. For this reason, keep the `Cache-Control` and `Expires` headers in mind, and be sure to set intentional values.

There are many more features available to service workers than those covered in this section. Mozilla, the company behind Firefox, was nice enough to put together a cookbook website full of common strategies when building out service workers. This website is available at *https://serviceworke.rs* and we recommend checking it out if you're considering implementing service workers in your next web app.

Service workers, and the other web workers you've looked at, certainly come with a bit of complexity. Lucky for us, there are some convenient libraries available, and communication patterns that you can implement, to make managing them a little easier.

Cross-Document Communication

There are other ways to employ multithreaded JavaScript programming in browsers without needing to instantiate a web worker. These can be done by communicating across different browser contexts, both fully open pages and iframes. Browsers provide APIs to allow for communication across these pages.

The first approach works by embedding iframes in a web page, or by creating a pop-up window, and has been available before web workers existed. The parent window is able to get a reference to the child window and can then call a `.postMessage()` method on that reference to send messages to the child. The child window can then listen for `message` events on its `window` object. The child can also pass messages back to the parent window. This pattern likely inspired the web worker interfaces.

The second approach is a bit more universal. It allows for communication across not only pop-ups and iframes but also any window that is opened for the same origin. It goes even further and allows for communication across worker threads as well. This

---

communication is achieved by instantiating a new `BroadcastChannel` instance, passing in the name of a channel as the first argument. This channel then allows for pub/sub (publish and subscribe) communication. The resulting object has a `.postMessage()` method and can have an `.onmessage` handler assigned. All objects that are listening on this channel across different environments will all have their message handler called when a message has been posted. The instance also has a `.close()` method to disconnect the instance from the channel.

Message Passing Abstractions

Each of the web workers covered in this chapter expose an interface for passing messages into, and receiving messages from, a separate JavaScript environment. This allows you to build applications that are capable of running JavaScript simultaneously across multiple cores.

However, you've really only worked with simple, contrived examples so far, passing along simple strings and calling simple functions. When it comes to building larger applications it'll be important to pass messages along that can scale and run code in workers that can scale, and simplifying the interface when working with workers will also reduce potential errors.

The RPC Pattern

So far, you've only worked with passing basic strings along to workers. While this is fine for getting a feel for the capabilities of web workers, it's something that isn't going to scale well for a full application.

For example, let's assume you have a web worker that does a single thing, like sum all the square root values from 1 to 1,000,000. Well, you could just call the `postMessage()` for the worker, without passing arguments, then run the slow logic in the `onmessage` handler, and send the message back using the worker's `postMessage()` function. But what if the worker also needs to calculate Fibonacci sequence? In that case you could pass in a string, one for `square_sum`, and one for `fibonacci`. But what if you need arguments? Well, you could pass in `square_sum|1000000`. But what if you need argument types? Maybe you get something like `square_sum|num:1000000`. You can probably see what we're getting at.

The RPC (Remote Procedure Call) pattern is a way to take a representation of a function and its arguments, serialize them, and pass them to a remote destination to have them get executed. The string `square_sum|num:1000000` is actually a form of RPC that we accidentally recreated. Perhaps it could ultimately translate into a function call like `squareNum(1000000)`, which is considered in "The Command Dispatcher Pattern" on page 45.

There's another bit of complexity that an application needs to worry about as well. If the main thread only sends a single message to a web worker at a time, then when a message is returned from the web worker, you know it's the response to the message. But if you send multiple messages to a web worker at the same time, there's no easy way to correlate the responses. For example, imagine an application that sends two messages to a web worker and receives two responses:

```
worker.postMessage('square_sum|num:4');
worker.postMessage('fibonacci|num:33');

worker.onmessage = (result) => {
  // Which result belongs to which message?
  // '3524578'
  // 4.1462643
};
```

Luckily, there does exist a standard for passing messages around and fulfilling the RPC pattern that inspiration can be drawn from. This standard is called JSON-RPC (*https://jsonrpc.org*), and it's fairly trivial to implement. This standard defines JSON representations of request and response objects as "notification" objects, a way to define the method being called and arguments in the request, the result in the response, and a mechanism for associating requests and responses. It even supports error values and batching of requests. For this example you'll only work with a request and response.

Taking the two function calls from our example, the JSON-RPC version of those requests and responses might look like this:

```
// worker.postMessage
{"jsonrpc": "2.0", "method": "square_sum", "params": [4], "id": 1}
{"jsonrpc": "2.0", "method": "fibonacci", "params": [33], "id": 2}

// worker.onmessage
{"jsonrpc": "2.0", "result": "3524578", "id": 2}
{"jsonrpc": "2.0", "result": 4.1462643, "id": 1}
```

In this case there's now a clear correlation between the response messages and their request.

JSON-RPC is intended to use JSON as the encoding when serializing messages, particularly when sending messages over the network. In fact, those `jsonrpc` fields define the version of JSON-RPC that the message is adhering to, which is very important in a network setting. However, because web workers use the structured clone algorithm (covered in the Appendix) that allows passing JSON-compatible objects along, an app could just pass objects directly without paying the cost of JSON serialization and deserialization. Also, the `jsonrpc` fields might not be as important in the browser where you have tighter control of both ends of the communication channel.

With these id properties correlating request and response objects, it's possible to then correlate which message relates to which. You'll build a solution for correlating these two in "Putting It All Together" on page 47. But, for now, you need to first determine which function to call when a message is received.

The Command Dispatcher Pattern

While the RPC pattern is useful for defining protocols, it doesn't necessarily provide a mechanism for determining what code path to execute on the receiving end. The command dispatcher pattern solves this, providing a way to take a serialized command, find the appropriate function, and then execute it, optionally passing in arguments.

This pattern is fairly straightforward to implement and doesn't require a whole lot of magic. First, we can assume that there are two variables that contain relevant information about the method or *command* that the code needs to run. The first variable is called method and is a string. The second variable is called args and is an array of values to be passed into the method. Assume these have been pulled from the RPC layer of the application.

The code that ultimately needs to run might live in different parts of the application. For example, maybe the square sum code lives in a third-party library, and the Fibonacci code is something that you've declared more locally. Regardless of where that code lives, you'll want to make a single repository that maps these commands to the code that needs to be run. There are several ways to pull this off, for example by using a Map object, but because the commands are going to be fairly static, a humble JavaScript object will suffice.

Another important concept is that only defined commands should be executed. If the caller wants to invoke a method that doesn't exist, an error should be gracefully generated that can be returned to the caller, without crashing the web worker. And, while the arguments could be passed into the method as an array, it would be a much nicer interface if the array of arguments were spread out into normal function arguments.

Example 2-11 shows an example implementation of a command dispatcher that you can use in your applications.

Example 2-11. Example command dispatcher

```
const commands = { ❶
  square_sum(max) {
    let sum = 0;
    for (let i = 0; i < max; i++) sum += Math.sqrt(i);
    return sum;
  },
  fibonacci(limit) {
```

```
    let prev = 1n, next = 0n, swap;
    while (limit) {
      swap = prev; prev = prev + next;
      next = swap; limit--;
    }
    return String(next);
  }
};
function dispatch(method, args) {
  if (commands.hasOwnProperty(method)) { ❷
    return commands[method](...args); ❸
  }
  throw new TypeError(`Command ${method} not defined!`);
}
```

❶ The definition of all supported commands.

❷ Check to see if command exists.

❸ Arguments are spread and method is invoked.

This code defines an object named commands that contains the entire collection of commands that are supported by the command dispatcher. In this case the code is inlined but it's absolutely fine, and even encouraged, to reach out to code that lives elsewhere.

The dispatch() function takes two arguments, the first being the name of the method and the second being the array of arguments. This function can be invoked when the web worker receives an RPC message representing the command. Within this function the first step is to check if the method exists. This is done using commands.hasOwnProperty(). This is much safer than calling method in commands or even commands[method] since you don't want noncommand properties like __proto__ being called.

If the command is determined to exist, then the command arguments are spread out, with the first array element being the first argument, etc. The function is then called with the arguments, with the result of the call being returned. However, if the command doesn't exist, then a TypeError is thrown.

This is about as basic of a command dispatcher as you can create. Other, more advanced dispatchers might do things like type checking, where the arguments are validated to adhere to a certain primitive type or where objects follow the appropriate shape, throwing errors generically so that the command method code doesn't need to do it.

These two patterns will definitely help your applications out, but the interface can be streamlined even more.

Putting It All Together

With JavaScript applications, we often think about performing work with outside services. For example, maybe we make a call to a database or maybe we make an HTTP request. When this happens we need to wait for a response to happen. Ideally, we can either provide a callback or treat this lookup as a promise. Although the web worker messaging interface doesn't make this straightforward, we can definitely build it out by hand.

It would also be nice to have a more symmetrical interface within a web worker, perhaps by making use of an asynchronous function, one where the resolved value is automatically sent back to the calling environment, without the need to manually call `postMessage()` within the code.

In this section, you'll do just that. You'll combine the RPC pattern and the command dispatcher pattern and end up with an interface that makes working with web workers much like working with other external libraries you may be more familiar with. This example uses a dedicated worker, but the same thing could be built with a shared worker or service worker.

First, create a new directory named *ch2-patterns/* to house the files you're going to create. In here first create another basic HTML file named *index.html* containing the contents of Example 2-12.

Example 2-12. ch2-patterns/index.html

```
<html>
  <head>
    <title>Worker Patterns</title>
    <script src="rpc-worker.js"></script>
    <script src="main.js"></script>
  </head>
</html>
```

This time the file is loading two JavaScript files. The first is a new library, and the second is the main JavaScript file, which you'll now create. Make a file named *main.js*, and add the contents of Example 2-13 to it.

Example 2-13. ch2-patterns/main.js

```
const worker = new RpcWorker('worker.js');

Promise.allSettled([
  worker.exec('square_sum', 1_000_000),
  worker.exec('fibonacci', 1_000),
  worker.exec('fake_method'),
  worker.exec('bad'),
```

```
]).then((([square_sum, fibonacci, fake, bad]) => {
  console.log('square sum', square_sum);
  console.log('fibonacci', fibonacci);
  console.log('fake', fake);
  console.log('bad', bad);
});
```

This file represents application code using these new design patterns. First, a worker instance is created, but not by calling one of the web worker classes you've been working with so far. Instead, the code instantiates a new RpcWorker class. This class is going to be defined soon.

After that, four calls to different RPC methods are made by calling worker.exec. The first one is a call to the square_sum method, the second is to the fibonacci method, the third is to a method that doesn't exist called fake_method, and the fourth is to a failing method named bad. The first argument is the name of the method, and all the following arguments end up being the arguments that are passed to the method.

The exec method returns a promise, one that will resolve if the operation succeeds and will reject if the operation fails. With this in mind, each of the promises has been wrapped into a single Promise.allSettled() call. This will run all of them and then continue the execution once each is complete—regardless of success or failure. After that the result of each operation is printed. allSettled() results include an array of objects with a status string property, and either a value or reason property depending on success or failure.

Next, create a file named *rpc-worker.js*, and add the contents of Example 2-14 to it.

Example 2-14. ch2-patterns/rpc-worker.js (part 1)

```
class RpcWorker {
  constructor(path) {
    this.next_command_id = 0;
    this.in_flight_commands = new Map();
    this.worker = new Worker(path);
    this.worker.onmessage = this.onMessageHandler.bind(this);
  }
}
```

This first part of the file starts the RpcWorker class and defines the constructor. Within the constructor a few properties are initialized. First, the next_command_id is set to zero. This value is used as the JSON-RPC-style incrementing message identifier. This is used to correlate the request and response objects.

Next, a property named in_flight_commands is initialized to an empty Map. This contains entries keyed by the command ID, with a value that contains a promise's resolve and reject functions. The size of this map grows with the number of parallel messages sent to the worker and shrinks as their correlating messages are returned.

After that, a dedicated worker is instantiated and assigned to the worker property. This class effectively encapsulates a Worker instance. After that the onmessage handler of the worker is configured to call the onMessageHandler for the class (defined in the next chunk of code). The RpcWorker class doesn't extend Worker because it doesn't really want to expose functionality of the underlying web worker, instead creating a completely new interface.

Continue modifying the file by adding the content from Example 2-15 to it.

Example 2-15. ch2-patterns/rpc-worker.js (part 2)

```
onMessageHandler(msg) {
  const { result, error, id } = msg.data;
  const { resolve, reject } = this.in_flight_commands.get(id);
  this.in_flight_commands.delete(id);
  if (error) reject(error);
  else resolve(result);
}
```

This chunk of the file defines the onMessageHandler method, which runs when the dedicated worker posts a message. This code assumes that a JSON-RPC-like message is passed from the web worker to the calling environment, and so, it first extracts the result, error, and id values from the response.

Next, it consults the in_flight_commands map to find the matching id value, retrieving the appropriate rejection and resolving functions, deleting the entry from the list in the process. If the error value was provided, then the operation is considered a failure and the reject() function is called with the erroneous value. Otherwise, the resolve() function is called with the result of the operation. Note that this doesn't support throwing falsy values.

For a production-ready version of this library you would also want to support a timeout value for these operations. Theoretically, it's possible for an error to be thrown in such a way, or for a promise to never end up resolving in the worker, and the calling environment would want to reject the promise and also clear the data from the map. Otherwise the application might end up with a memory leak.

Finally, finish up this file by adding the remaining content from Example 2-16 to it.

Example 2-16. ch2-patterns/rpc-worker.js (part 3)

```
exec(method, ...args) {
  const id = ++this.next_command_id;
  let resolve, reject;
  const promise = new Promise((res, rej) => {
    resolve = res;
    reject = rej;
```

```
  });
  this.in_flight_commands.set(id, { resolve, reject });
  this.worker.postMessage({ method, params: args, id });
  return promise;
  }
}
```

This last chunk of the file defines the exec() method, which is called when the application wants to execute a method in the web worker. The first thing that happens is that a new id value is generated. Next, a promise is created, which will later be returned by the method. The reject and resolve functions for the promise are pulled out and are added to the in_flight_commands map, associated with the id value.

After that, a message is posted to the worker. The object that is passed into the worker is an object roughly adhering to the JSON-RPC shape. It contains the method property, a params property that is the remaining arguments in an array, and the id value that was generated for this particular command execution.

This is a fairly common pattern, useful for associating outgoing asynchronous messages with incoming asynchronous messages. You might find yourself implementing a similar pattern if you needed to, say, put a message onto a network queue and later receive a message. But, again, it does have memory implications.

With the RPC worker file out of the way, you're ready to create the last file. Make a file named *worker.js*, and add the contents of Example 2-17 to it.

Example 2-17. ch2-patterns/worker.js

```
const sleep = (ms) => new Promise((res) => setTimeout(res, ms));  ❶

function asyncOnMessageWrap(fn) {  ❷
  return async function(msg) {
    postMessage(await fn(msg.data));
  }
}

const commands = {
  async square_sum(max) {
    await sleep(Math.random() * 100);  ❸
    let sum = 0; for (let i = 0; i < max; i++) sum += Math.sqrt(i);
    return sum;
  },
  async fibonacci(limit) {
    await sleep(Math.random() * 100);
    let prev = 1n, next = 0n, swap;
    while (limit) { swap = prev; prev = prev + next; next = swap; limit--; }
    return String(next);  ❹
  },
```

```
  async bad() {
    await sleep(Math.random() * 10);
    throw new Error('oh no');
  }
};

self.onmessage = asyncOnMessageWrap(async (rpc) => { ❺
  const { method, params, id } = rpc;

  if (commands.hasOwnProperty(method)) {
    try {
      const result = await commands[method](...params);
      return { id, result }; ❻
    } catch (err) {
      return { id, error: { code: -32000, message: err.message }};
    }
  } else {
    return { ❼
      id, error: {
        code: -32601,
        message: `method ${method} not found`
      }
    };
  }
});
```

❶   Adds artificial slowdown to methods.

❷   A basic wrapper to convert onmessage to an async function.

❸   Artificial random slowdowns are added to the commands.

❹   The BigInt result is coerced into a JSON-friendly string value.

❺   The onmessage wrapper is injected.

❻   A successful JSON-RPC-like message is resolved on success.

❼   An erroneous JSON-RPC-like message is rejected if a method doesn't exist.

This file has a lot going on. First, the sleep function is just a promise equivalent version of setTimeout(). The asyncOnMessageWrap() is a function that can wrap an async function and be assigned the onmessage handler. This is a convenience to pull out the data property of the incoming message, pass it to the function, await the result, then pass the result to postMessage().

After that, the `commands` object from before has made its return. This time, though, artificial timeouts have been added and the functions have been made into `async` functions. This lets the methods emulate an otherwise slow asynchronous process.

Finally, the `onmessage` handler is assigned using the wrapper function. The code inside it takes the incoming JSON-RPC-like message and pulls out the `method`, `params`, and `id` properties. Much like before, the commands collection is consulted to see if it has the method. If it doesn't, a JSON-RPC-like error is returned. The `-32601` value is a magic number defined by JSON-RPC to represent a method that doesn't exist. When the command does exist, the command method is executed, then the resolved value is coerced into a JSON-RPC-like successful message and returned. If the command throws, then a different error is returned, using another JSON-RPC magic number of `-32000`.

Once you've got the file created, switch to your browser and open the inspector. Then, launch the web server again using the following command from within the *ch2-patterns/* directory:

```
$ npx serve .
```

Next, switch back to browser and paste in the URL from the output. You won't see anything interesting on the page, but in the console you should see the following messages:

```
square sum      { status: "fulfilled", value: 666666166.4588418 }
fibonacci       { status: "fulfilled", value: "4346655768..." }
fake            { status: "rejected", reason: { code: -32601,
                  message: "method fake_method not found" } }
bad             { status: "rejected", reason: { code: -32000,
                  message: "oh no" } }
```

In this case you can see that both the `square_sum` and `fibonacci` calls ended successfully, while the `fake_method` command resulted in failure. More importantly, under the hood, the calls to the methods are resolving in different orders, but thanks to the incrementing `id` values the responses are always properly correlated to their requests.

## CHAPTER 3

Node.js

Outside browsers, there's only one JavaScript runtime of note, and that's *Node.js*.[1] Although it started as a platform emphasizing single-threaded concurrency in servers with continuation-passing style callbacks, a lot of effort went into making it a general-purpose programming platform.

Many tasks performed by Node.js programs don't fit into its traditional use case of serving web requests or handling network connections. Instead, a lot of newer Node.js programs are command-line tools acting as build systems, or parts of them, for JavaScript. Such programs are typically heavy on I/O operations, just like servers are, but they also typically do a lot of data processing.

For example, tools like Babel (*https://babeljs.io*) and TypeScript (*https://typescript lang.org*) will transform your code from one language (or language version) to another. Tools like Webpack (*https://webpack.js.org*), Rollup (*https://rollupjs.org*), and Parcel (*https://parceljs.org*) will bundle and minify your code for distribution to your web frontend or to other environments where load times are crucial, like serverless environments. In situations like these, while there's a lot of filesystem I/O going on, there's also a lot of data processing, which is generally done synchronously. These are the sorts of situations where parallelism is handy and might get the job done quicker.

Parallelism can also be useful in the original Node.js use case, which is servers. Data processing may happen a lot, depending on your application. For example, *server side rendering (SSR)* involves a lot of string manipulation where the source data is already known. This is one of many examples where we might want to add parallelism to

---

1 Yes, other nonbrowser JavaScript runtimes exist, like Deno, but Node.js has such a massive amount of popularity and market share at time of writing that it's the only one worth talking about here. This may change by the time you're reading this, and that's great for the world of JavaScript! Hopefully, there's a newer edition of this book that covers your nonbrowser JavaScript runtime of choice.

our solutions. "When to Use" on page 176 examines a situation where parallelism improves template rendering time.

Today, we have `worker_threads` for parallelizing our code. This wasn't always the case, but that didn't mean we were limited to single-threaded concurrency.

Before We Had Threads

Prior to threads being available in Node.js, if you wanted to take advantage of CPU cores, you needed to use processes. As discussed in Chapter 1, we don't get some of the benefits we'd get from threads if we use processes. That being said, if shared memory isn't important (and in many cases it isn't!) then processes are perfectly able to solve these kinds of problems for you.

Consider Figure 1-1 from Chapter 1. In that scenario, we have threads responding to HTTP requests sent to them from a main thread, which is listening on a port. While this concept is great for handling traffic from several CPU cores, we can also use processes to achieve a similar effect. It might look something like Figure 3-1.

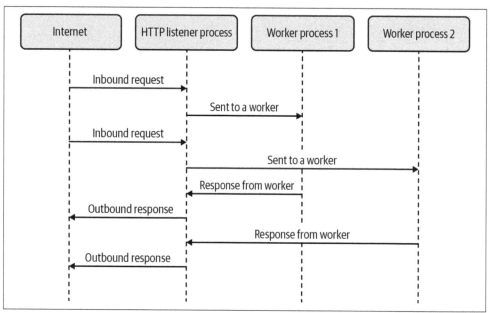

Figure 3-1. Processes as they might be used in an HTTP server

Although we could do something like this using the `child_process` API in Node.js, we're better off using `cluster`, which was purpose-built for this use case. This module's purpose is to spread network traffic across several worker processes. Let's go ahead and use it in a simple "Hello, World" example.

The code in Example 3-1 is a standard HTTP server in Node.js. It simply responds to any request, regardless of path or method, with "Hello, World!" followed by a new line character.

Example 3-1. A "Hello, World" server in Node.js

```
const http = require('http');

http.createServer((req, res) => {
  res.end('Hello, World!\n');
}).listen(3000);
```

Now, let's add four processes with `cluster`. With the `cluster` module, the common approach is to use an `if` block to detect whether we're in the main listening process or one of the worker processes. If we're in the main process, then we have to do the work of spawning the worker processes. Otherwise, we just set up an ordinary web server as before in each of the workers. This should look something like Example 3-2.

Example 3-2. A "Hello, World" server in Node.js using `cluster`

```
const http = require('http');
const cluster = require('cluster'); ❶

if (cluster.isPrimary) { ❷
  cluster.fork(); ❸
  cluster.fork();
  cluster.fork();
  cluster.fork();
} else {
  http.createServer((req, res) => {
    res.end('Hello, World!\n');
  }).listen(3000); ❹
}
```

❶ Require the `cluster` module.

❷ Change code paths depending on whether we're in the primary process.

❸ In the primary process, create four worker processes.

❹ In the worker processes, create a web server and listen, like in Example 3-1.

You may notice that we're creating web servers that listen on the same port in four difference processes. It seems like a mistake. After all, if we try to bind a server to a port that's already being used, we usually get an error. Don't worry! We're not actually listening on the same port four times. It turns out Node.js does some magic for us in `cluster`.

When worker processes are set up in a cluster, any call to `listen()` will actually cause Node.js to listen on the primary process rather than on the worker. Then, once a connection is received in the primary process, it's handed off to a worker process via IPC. On most systems, this happens on a round-robin basis. This somewhat convoluted system is how each worker can *appear* to be listening on the same port, when in fact it's just the primary process listening on that port and passing connections off to all the workers.

 Historically, the `isPrimary` property on `cluster` used to be called `isMaster`, and for compatibility reasons, it's still there as an alias at time of writing. The change was introduced in Node.js v16.0.0.

This change was made in an effort to reduce the amount of potentially harmful language in Node.js. The project aims to be a welcoming community, and words with a given usage that are rooted in a history of slavery are antithetical to that goal.

Processes incur some extra overhead that threads don't, and we also don't get shared memory, which helps with faster transfer of data. For that, we need the `worker_threads` module.

The worker_threads Module

Node.js's support for threads is in a built-in module called `worker_threads`. It provides an interface to threads that mimics a lot of what you'd find in web browsers for web workers. Since Node.js is not a web browser, not all the APIs are the same, and the environment inside these worker threads isn't the same as what you'd find inside web workers.

Instead, inside Node.js worker threads you'll find the usual Node.js API available via `require`, or `import` if you're using ESM. There are a few differences in the API compared to the main thread though:

- You can't exit the program with `process.exit()`. Instead this will just exit the thread.

- You can't change working directories with `process.chdir()`. In fact, this function is not even available.

- You can't handle signals with `process.on()`.

Another important thing to note is that the `libuv` worker pool is shared across worker threads. Recall "Hidden Threads" on page 9, where it was noted that the libuv thread pool consists of a default of four threads to create nonblocking interfaces to low-level blocking APIs. If you're finding yourself bound by that thread pool's size (due to, for example, a lot of filesystem I/O), you'll find that adding more threads via `worker_threads` won't lighten the load. Instead, apart from considering various caching solutions and other optimizations, consider increasing your `UV_THREAD POOL_SIZE`. Likewise, you might find that you have little choice but to increase this when adding JavaScript threads via the `worker_threads` module, due to their usage of the `libuv` thread pool.

There are other caveats too, so you're encouraged to have a look at the Node.js documentation (*https://oreil.ly/CYxtz*) for a full list of differences for your particular version of Node.js.

You can create a new worker thread by using the `Worker` constructor, like in Example 3-3.

Example 3-3. Spawning a new worker thread in Node.js

```
const { Worker } = require('worker_threads');

const worker = new Worker('/path/to/worker-file-name.js'); ❶
```

❶ The filename here is the entrypoint file that we want to run inside the worker thread. This is similar to the entrypoint in the main file that we'd specify as an argument to `node` on the command line.

workerData

It's not sufficient to just be able to create a worker thread. We need to interact with it! The `Worker` constructor takes a second argument, an `options` object, that among other things allows us to specify a set of data to be passed immediately to the worker thread. The `options` object property is called `workerData`, and its contents will be copied into the worker thread via the means described in the Appendix. Inside the thread, we can access the cloned data via the `workerData` property of the `worker_threads` module. You can see how this works in Example 3-4.

Example 3-4. Passing data to a worker thread via `workerData`

```
const {
  Worker,
  isMainThread,
  workerData
} = require('worker_threads');
const assert = require('assert');
```

```
if (isMainThread) { ❶
  const worker = new Worker(__filename, { workerData: { num: 42 } });
} else {
  assert.strictEqual(workerData.num, 42);
}
```

❶ Rather than using a separate file for the worker thread, we can use the current file with __filename and switch the behavior based on isMainThread.

It's important to note that the properties of the workerData object are *cloned* rather than shared between threads. Unlike in C, shared memory in JavaScript threads does not mean all the variables are visible. This means any changes you make in that object will not be visible in the other thread. They are separate objects. That being said, you can have memory that's shared between threads via SharedArrayBuffer. These can be shared via workerData or by being sent through a MessagePort, which is covered in the next section. Additionally, SharedArrayBuffer is covered in depth in Chapter 4.

MessagePort

A MessagePort is one end of a two-way data stream. By default, one is provided to every worker thread to provide a communication channel to and from the main thread. It's available in the worker thread as the parentPort property of the worker_threads module.

To send a message via the port, the postMesage() method is called on it. The first argument is any object that can be passed, as described in the Appendix, which will end up being the message data being passed to the other end of the port. When a message is received on the port, the message event is fired, with the message data being the first argument to the event handler function. In the main thread, the event and the postMessage() method are on the worker instance itself, rather than having to get them from a MessagePort instance. Example 3-5 shows a simple example where messages sent to the main thread are echoed back to a worker thread.

Example 3-5. Bidirectional communication via the default MessagePorts

```
const {
  Worker,
  isMainThread,
  parentPort
} = require('worker_threads');

if (isMainThread) {
  const worker = new Worker(__filename);
  worker.on('message', msg => {
    worker.postMessage(msg);
```

```
  });
} else {
  parentPort.on('message', msg => {
    console.log('We got a message from the main thread:', msg);
  });
  parentPort.postMessage('Hello, World!');
}
```

You can also create a pair of `MessagePort` instances connected to each other via the `MessageChannel` constructor. You can then pass one of the ports via an existing message port (like the default one) or via `workerData`. You might want to do this in situations where neither of two threads that need to communicate are the main thread, or even just for organizational purposes. Example 3-6 is the same as the previous example, except using ports created via `MessageChannel` and passed via `workerData`.

Example 3-6. Bidirectional communication via `MessagePort` created with `MessageChannel`

```
const {
  Worker,
  isMainThread,
  MessageChannel,
  workerData
} = require('worker_threads');

if (isMainThread) {
  const { port1, port2 } = new MessageChannel();
  const worker = new Worker(__filename, {
    workerData: {
      port: port2
    },
    transferList: [port2]
  });
  port1.on('message', msg => {
    port1.postMessage(msg);
  });
} else {
  const { port } = workerData;
  port.on('message', msg => {
    console.log('We got a message from the main thread:', msg);
  });
  port.postMessage('Hello, World!');
}
```

You'll notice we used the `transferList` option when instantiating the `Worker`. This is a way of transferring ownership of objects from one thread to another. This is required when sending any `MessagePort`, `ArrayBuffer`, or `FileHandle` objects via `workerData` or `postMessage`. Once these objects are transferred, they can no longer be used on the sending side.

 In more recent versions of Node.js, Web Hypertext Application Technology Working Group (WHATWG) `ReadableStream` and `WritableStream` are available. You can learn more about them in the Node.js documentation (*https://oreil.ly/TRJf0*) and in use by some APIs. They can be transferred via `transferList` over `Messa gePorts` to enable another way of communicating across threads. Under the hood, these are implemented using a `MessagePort` to send data across.

Happycoin: Revisited

Now that we've seen the basics of spawning threads in Node.js and having them communicate with each other, we have enough to rebuild our example from "Threads in C: Get Rich with Happycoin" on page 10 in Node.js.

Recall that Happycoin is our imaginary cryptocurrency, with a completely ridiculous proof-of-work algorithm that goes as follows:

1. Generate a random unsigned 64-bit integer.

2. Determine whether or not the integer is happy.

3. If it's not happy, it's not a Happycoin.

4. If it's not divisible by 10,000, it's not a Happycoin.

5. Otherwise, it's a Happycoin.

Much like we did in C, we'll make a single-threaded version first, and then adapt the code to run on multiple threads.

With Only the Main Thread

Let's start with generating random numbers. First, let's create a file called *happycoin.js*, in a directory called *ch3-happycoin/*. Fill it with the contents of Example 3-7.

Example 3-7. ch3-happycoin/happycoin.js

```
const crypto = require('crypto');

const big64arr = new BigUint64Array(1)
function random64() {
  crypto.randomFillSync(big64arr);
  return big64arr[0];
}
```

They crypto module in Node.js gives us some handy functions for getting cryptographically secure random numbers. We'll definitely want this since we're building a cryptocurrency after all! Luckily, it's less of an ordeal than it is in C.

The randomFillSync function fills a given TypedArray with random data. Since we're looking for only a single 64-bit unsigned integer, we can use a BigUint64Array. This particular TypedArray, along with its cousin BigInt64Array, are recent additions to JavaScript that were made possible by the new bigint type, which stores arbitrarily large integers. Returning the first (and only) element of this array after we've filled it with random data gives us the random 64-bit unsigned integer that we're looking for.

Now let's add our happy number calculation. Add the contents of Example 3-8 to your file.

Example 3-8. ch3-happycoin/happycoin.js

```
function sumDigitsSquared(num) {
  let total = 0n;
  while (num > 0) {
    const numModBase = num % 10n;
    total += numModBase ** 2n;
    num = num / 10n;
  }
  return total;
}

function isHappy(num) {
  while (num != 1n && num != 4n) {
    num = sumDigitsSquared(num);
  }
  return num === 1n;
}

function isHappycoin(num) {
  return isHappy(num) && num % 10000n === 0n;
}
```

These three functions, sumDigitsSquared, isHappy, and isHappycoin, are direct translations from their C counterparts in "Threads in C: Get Rich with Happycoin" on page 10. One thing you might notice if you're not familiar with bigint is the n suffix on all the number literals in this code. This suffix tells JavaScript that these numbers are to be treated as bigint values, rather than values of type number. This is important because, while both types support mathematical operators like +, -, **, and so on, they cannot interoperate without doing an explicit conversion. For example, 1 + 1n would be invalid because it's an attempt to add the number 1 to the bigint 1.

Let's finish off the file by implementing our Happycoin mining loop and outputting the count of found Happycoins. Add Example 3-9 to your file.

Example 3-9. ch3-happycoin/happycoin.js

```
let count = 0;
for (let i = 1; i < 10_000_000; i++) {
  const randomNum = random64();
  if (isHappycoin(randomNum)) {
    process.stdout.write(randomNum.toString() + ' ');
    count++;
  }
}

process.stdout.write('\ncount ' + count + '\n');
```

The code here is very similar to what we did in C. We loop 10,000,000 times, getting a random number and checking if it's a Happycoin. If it is, we print it out. Note that we're not using `console.log()` here because we don't want to insert a newline character after each number found. Instead we want spaces, so we're writing to the output stream directly. When we output the count after the loop, we need an additional newline character at the beginning of the output to separate it from the numbers above.

To run this program, use the following command in your *ch3-happycoin* directory:

```
$ node happycoin.js
```

Your output should be exactly the same as it was in C. That is, it should look something like this:

```
5503819098300300000 ... [ 125 more entries ] ... 5273033273820010000
count 127
```

This takes quite a bit longer than the C example. On a run-of-the-mill machine, this took about 1 minute and 45 seconds with Node.js v16.0.0.

There are a variety of reasons why this takes so much longer. When building applications and optimizing for performance, it's important to figure out what the sources of performance overhead are. Yes, in general, JavaScript is often "slower than C," but this enormous difference can't be explained by that alone. Yes, we'll get better performance in the next section when we split this into multiple threads of work, but as you'll see, it's not nearly enough to make this implementation compelling when compared to the C example.

And on that note, let's see what this looks like when we use `worker_threads` to split out the load.

With Four Worker Threads

To add worker threads, we will start from the code we had. Copy the contents of *happycoin.js* to *happycoin-threads.js*. Then insert the contents of Example 3-10 at the very beginning of the file, before the existing content.

Example 3-10. ch3-happycoin/happycoin-threads.js

```
const {
  Worker,
  isMainThread,
  parentPort
} = require('worker_threads');
```

We'll need these parts of the worker_threads module, so we require them at the beginning. Now, replace everything from let count = 0; to the end of the file with Example 3-11.

Example 3-11. ch3-happycoin/happycoin-threads.js

```
const THREAD_COUNT = 4;

if (isMainThread) {
  let inFlight = THREAD_COUNT;
  let count = 0;
  for (let i = 0; i < THREAD_COUNT; i++) {
    const worker = new Worker(__filename);
    worker.on('message', msg => {
      if (msg === 'done') {
        if (--inFlight === 0) {
          process.stdout.write('\ncount ' + count + '\n');
        }
      } else if (typeof msg === 'bigint') {
        process.stdout.write(msg.toString() + ' ');
        count++;
      }
    })
  }
} else {
  for (let i = 1; i < 10_000_000/THREAD_COUNT; i++) {
    const randomNum = random64();
    if (isHappycoin(randomNum)) {
      parentPort.postMessage(randomNum);
    }
  }
  parentPort.postMessage('done');
}
```

We're splitting behavior here with an `if` block. If we're on the main thread, we start four worker threads using the current file. Remember, `__filename` is a string containing the path and name of the current file. We then add a message handler for that worker. In the message handler, if the message is simply `done`, then the worker has completed its work, and if all other workers are done, we'll output the count. If the message is a number, or more correctly, a `bigint`, then we assume it's a Happycoin, and we'll print it out and add it to the count like we did in the single-threaded example.

On the `else` side of the `if` block, we're running in one of the worker threads. In here, we'll do the same sort of loop as we did in the single-threaded example, except we're only looping 1/4 of the number of times we did before, since we're doing the same work across four threads. Also, rather than writing directly to the output stream, we're sending found Happycoins back to the main thread via the `MessagePort` given to us, called `parentPort`. We've already set up the handler on the main thread for this. When the loop exits, we send a `done` on the `parentPort` to indicate to the main thread that we won't be finding any more Happycoins on this thread.

We could have simply printed the Happycoins to the output immediately, but just like with the C example, we don't want the different threads to clobber each other in the output, so we need to *synchronize*. Chapters 4 and 5 go over more advanced techniques for synchronization, but for now it's enough to just send the data back to the main thread through the `parentPort` and let the main thread handle output.

Now that we're done adding threads to this example, you can run it with the following command in your *ch3-happycoin* directory:

```
$ node happycoin-threads.js
```

You should see output that looks something like this:

```
17241719184686550000 ... [ 137 more entries ] ... 17618203841507830000
count 139
```

Like with the C example, this code runs quite a bit faster. In a test on the same computer and Node.js version as the single-threaded example, it ran in about 33 seconds. This is a huge improvement over the single-threaded example, so another big win for threads!

 This is not the only way to split this kind of problem up for thread-based computation. For example, other synchronization techniques could be used to avoid passing data between threads, or the messages could be batched. Always be sure to test and compare to find out whether threads are an ideal solution and which thread techniques are most applicable to your problem, and the most efficient.

Worker Pools with Piscina

Many types of workloads will naturally lend themselves to using threads. In Node.js, most workloads involve processing an HTTP request. If within that code you find yourself doing a lot of math or synchronous data processing, it may make sense to offload that work to one or more threads. These types of operations involve submitting a single task to a thread and waiting for a result from it. In much the same way a threaded web server often works, it makes sense to maintain a pool of workers that can be sent various tasks from the main thread.

This section only takes a shallow look at thread pools, adapting the familiar Happycoins application and abstracting the pooling mechanism using a package. "Thread Pool" on page 121 covers thread pools extensively, building out an implementation from scratch.

The concept of pooled resources isn't unique to threads. For example, web browsers typically create pools of socket connections to web servers so that they can multiplex all the various HTTP requests required to render a web page across those connections. Database client libraries often do a similar thing with sockets connected to the database server.

There's a handy module available for Node.js called *generic-pool* (*https://oreil.ly/2a6ua*), which is a helper module for dealing with arbitrary pooled resources. These resources could be anything, like database connections, other sockets, local caches, threads, or pretty much anything else that might require having multiple instances of something but only accessing one at a time, without caring which one it is.

For the use case of discrete tasks sent to a pool of worker threads, we have the *piscina* (*https://oreil.ly/0p8zi*) module at our disposal. This module encapsulates the work of setting up a bunch of worker threads and allocating tasks to them. The name of the module comes from the Italian word for "pool."

The basic usage is straightforward. You create an instance of the `Piscina` class, passing in a `filename`, which will be used in the worker thread. Behind the scenes, a pool of worker threads is created, and a queue is set up to handle incoming tasks. You can enqueue a task by calling `.run()`, passing in a value containing all the data necessary to complete this task, and noting that the values will be cloned as they would be with `postMessage()`. This returns a promise that resolves once the tasks have been completed by a worker, giving a result value. In the file to be run in the worker, a function must be exported that takes in whatever is passed to `.run()` and returns the result value. This function can also be an `async` function, so that you can do asynchronous tasks in a worker thread if you need to. A basic example calculating square roots in worker threads is found in Example 3-12.

Example 3-12. Computing square roots with `piscina`

```
const Piscina = require('piscina');

if (!Piscina.isWorkerThread) { ❶
  const piscina = new Piscina({ filename: __filename }); ❷
  piscina.run(9).then(squareRootOfNine => { ❸
    console.log('The square root of nine is', squareRootOfNine);
  });
}

module.exports = num => Math.sqrt(num); ❹
```

❶ Much like `cluster` and `worker_threads`, `piscina` provides a handy boolean for determining whether we're in the main thread or a worker thread.

❷ We'll use the same technique for using the same file as we did with the Happy-coin example.

❸ Since `.run()` returns a promise, we can just call `.then()` on it.

❹ The exported function is used in the worker thread to perform the actual work. In this case, it's just calculating a square root.

While it's all fine and good to run one task on the pool, we need to be able to run *many* tasks on the pool. Let's say we want to calculate the square roots of every number less than ten million. Let's go ahead and loop ten million times. We'll also replace the logging with an assertion that we've gotten a numeric result, since logging will be quite noisy. Have a look at Example 3-13.

Example 3-13. Computing ten million square roots with `piscina`

```
const Piscina = require('piscina');
const assert = require('assert');

if (!Piscina.isWorkerThread) {
  const piscina = new Piscina({ filename: __filename });
  for (let i = 0; i < 10_000_000; i++) {
    piscina.run(i).then(squareRootOfI => {
      assert.ok(typeof squareRootOfI === 'number');
    });
  }
}
```

```
module.exports = num => Math.sqrt(num);
```

This seems like it ought to work. We're submitting ten million numbers to be processed by the worker pool. However, if you run this code, you'll get a nonrecoverable JavaScript memory allocation error. On one trial of this with Node.js v16.0.0, the following output was observed.

```
FATAL ERROR: Reached heap limit Allocation failed
    - JavaScript heap out of memory
 1: 0xb12b00 node::Abort() [node]
 2: 0xa2fe25 node::FatalError(char const*, char const*) [node]
 3: 0xcf8a9e v8::Utils::ReportOOMFailure(v8::internal::Isolate*,
    char const*, bool) [node]
 4: 0xcf8e17 v8::internal::V8::FatalProcessOutOfMemory(v8::internal::Isolate*,
    char const*, bool) [node]
 5: 0xee2d65  [node]
[ ... 13 more lines of a not-particularly-useful C++ stacktrace ... ]
Aborted (core dumped)
```

What's going on here? It turns out the underlying task queue is not infinite. By default, the task queue will keep growing and growing until we run into an allocation error like this one. To avoid having this happen, we need to set a reasonable limit. The piscina module lets you set a limit by using a maxQueue option in its constructor, which can be set to any positive integer. Through experimentation, the maintainers of piscina have found that an ideal maxQueue value is the square of the number of worker threads it's using. Handily, you can use this number without even knowing it by setting maxQueue to auto.

Once we've established a bound for the queue size, we need to be able to handle it when the queue is full. There are two ways to detect that the queue is full:

1. Compare the values of piscina.queueSize and piscina.options.maxQueue. If they're equal, then the queue is full. This can be done prior to calling piscina.run() to avoid attempting to enqueue when it's full. This is the recommended way to check.

2. If piscina.run() is called when the queue is full, the returned promise will reject with an error indicating that the queue is full. This isn't ideal because by this point we're already in a further tick of the event loop and many other attempts to enqueue may already have happened.

When we know that the queue is full, we need a way of knowing when it'll be ready for new tasks again. Fortunately, piscina pools emit a drain event once the queue is empty, which is certainly an ideal time to start adding new tasks. In Example 3-14, we put this all together with an async function around the loop that submits the tasks.

Example 3-14. Computing ten million square roots with `piscina`*, without crashing*

```
const Piscina = require('piscina');
const assert = require('assert');
const { once } = require('events');

if (!Piscina.isWorkerThread) {
  const piscina = new Piscina({
    filename: __filename,
    maxQueue: 'auto' ❶
  });
  (async () => { ❷
    for (let i = 0; i < 10_000_000; i++) {
      if (piscina.queueSize === piscina.options.maxQueue) { ❸
        await once(piscina, 'drain'); ❹
      }
      piscina.run(i).then(squareRootOfI => {
        assert.ok(typeof squareRootOfI === 'number');
      });
    }
  })();
}

module.exports = num => Math.sqrt(num);
```

❶ The `maxQueue` option is set to `auto`, which limits the queue size to the square of the number of threads that `piscina` is using.

❷ The `for` loop is wrapped in an `async` immediately invoked function expression (IIFE) in order to use an `await` within it.

❸ When this check is true, the queue is full.

❹ We then wait for the `drain` event before submitting any new tasks to the queue.

Running this code does *not* result in an out-of-memory crash like it did before. It takes a fairly long time to complete, but it does finally exit without issue.

As seen here, it's easy to fall into a trap where using a tool in what seems like the most sensible way isn't the best approach. It's important to fully understand tools like `piscina` when building out your multithreaded applications.

On that note, let's see what happens when we try to use `piscina` to mine Happycoins.

A Pool Full of Happycoins

To use `piscina` to produce Happycoins, we'll use a slightly different approach from what we did in the original `worker_threads` implementation. Instead of getting a message back every time we have a Happycoin, we'll batch them together and send them all at once when we're done. This trade-off saves us the effort of setting up a `MessageChannel` to send data back to the main thread with; the side effect is that we'll only get our results in batches, rather than as soon as they're ready. The main thread will still do the job of spawning the appropriate threads and retrieving all the results.

Trade-offs

All programming is about trade-offs. Multithreaded programming is no exception. In fact, you'll find trade-offs at every turn. Sacrificing convenience in one place will often give you performance gains elsewhere, or vice versa. Sometimes if one operation is slightly slower, another will be significantly faster.

As with all things, *measure*. You can think as hard as you want about the problem, but the surest way to know whether your trade-off is going to be worth it is to measure. Check your code in a variety of conditions and see if it behaves in a way that's actually beneficial in all the ways that matter. Crucially, the ways that matter are determined by the problem at hand, your interpretation of it, and the needs of your stakeholders.

In addition to measuring, documentation can save you hours, days, or even weeks of frustration in the future. It's a pain to make a trade-off and then months down the road being unsure what led to that decision and starting to question everything.

To start off, copy your *happycoin-threads.js* file to a new one called *happycoin-piscina.js*. We'll build off our old `worker_threads` example here. Now replace everything before the `require('crypto')` line with Example 3-15.

Example 3-15. ch3-happycoin/happycoin-piscina.js

```
const Piscina = require('piscina');
```

Yep, that's it! Now we'll get to the more substantial stuff. Replace everything after the `isHappycoin()` function declaration with the contents of Example 3-16.

Example 3-16. ch3-happycoin/happycoin-piscina.js

```
const THREAD_COUNT = 4;

if (!Piscina.isWorkerThread) { ❶
  const piscina = new Piscina({
    filename: __filename, ❷
    minThreads: THREAD_COUNT, ❸
    maxThreads: THREAD_COUNT
  });
  let done = 0;
  let count = 0;
  for (let i = 0; i < THREAD_COUNT; i++) { ❹
    (async () => {
      const { total, happycoins } = await piscina.run(); ❺
      process.stdout.write(happycoins);
      count += total;
      if (++done === THREAD_COUNT) { ❻
        console.log('\ncount', count);
      }
    })();
  }
}
```

❶ We'll use the isWorkerThread property to check that we're in the main thread.

❷ We're using the same technique as earlier to create worker threads using this same file.

❸ We want to restrict the number of threads to be exactly four, to match our previous examples. We'll want to time this and see what happens, so sticking with four threads reduces the number of variables here.

❹ We know we have four threads, so we'll enqueue our task four times. Each one will complete once it has checked its chunk of random numbers for Happycoins.

❺ We submit the task to the queue in this async IIFE, so that they all get queued in the same event loop iteration. Don't worry, we won't get out-of-memory errors like we did before because we know we have exactly four threads and we're only enqueueing four tasks. As we'll see later, the task returns both the output string and the total count of Happycoins that the thread has found.

❻ Much like we've done in previous Happycoin implementations, we'll check that all threads have completed their tasks before outputting the grand total count of Happycoins that we've found.

Next we'll add the code from Example 3-17, which adds the exported function that's used in `piscina`'s worker threads.

Example 3-17. ch3-happycoin/happycoin-piscina.js

```
module.exports = () => {
  let happycoins = '';
  let total = 0;
  for (let i = 0; i < 10_000_000/THREAD_COUNT; i++) { ❶
    const randomNum = random64();
    if (isHappycoin(randomNum)) {
      happycoins += randomNum.toString() + ' ';
      total++;
    }
  }
  return { total, happycoins }; ❷
}
```

❶ We're doing our typical Happycoin-hunting loop here, but as in other parallelism examples, we're dividing our total search space by the number of threads.

❷ We're passing the string of found Happycoins and the total count of them back to the main thread by returning a value from this function.

To run this, you'll have to install `piscina` if you haven't done so yet for the earlier examples. You can use the following two commands in your *ch3-happycoin* directory to set up a Node.js project and add the `piscina` dependency. The third line can then be used to run the code:

```
$ npm init -y
$ npm install piscina
$ node happycoin-piscina.js
```

You should see output the same as earlier examples, with a slight twist. Rather than seeing each Happycoin come in one by one, you'll see them either roughly all at once, or in four large groupings of them. This is the trade-off we made by returning the whole strings rather than the Happycoins one by one. This code should run in roughly the same time as *happycoin-threads.js*, since it uses the same principle, but with the abstraction layer that `piscina` provides us.

You can see that we're not using `piscina` in the typical manner. We're not passing it a multitude of discrete tasks that end up requiring careful queueing. The primary reason for this is performance.

If, for example, we had a loop iterating ten million times in the main thread, each time adding another task to the queue and `await`-ing its response, it would end up being just as slow as running all the code synchronously on the main thread. We could *not* await the reply and just add things to the queue as soon as we can, but it turns out the overhead of passing messages 20 million times is a lot greater than simply passing eight messages.

When dealing with raw data, like numbers or byte streams, there are usually faster ways of transferring data between threads using `SharedArrayBuffers`, and we'll see more about those in the next chapter.

## CHAPTER 4

Shared Memory

So far you've been exposed to the web workers API for browsers, covered in Chapter 2, and the worker threads module for Node.js, covered in "The worker_threads Module" on page 56. These are two powerful tools for working with concurrency in JavaScript, allowing developers to run code in parallel in a way that wasn't previously available to JavaScript.

However, the interaction you've had with them so far has been fairly shallow. While it's true they allow you to run code in parallel, you've only done so using message-passing APIs, ultimately depending on the familiar event loop to handle the receipt of a message. This is a much less performant system than the threading code you worked with in "Threads in C: Get Rich with Happycoin" on page 10 where these disparate threads are able to access the same shared memory.

This chapter covers two powerful tools available to your JavaScript applications: the `Atomics` object and the `SharedArrayBuffer` class. These allow you to share memory between two threads without depending on message passing. But before diving into a complete technical explanation for these objects, a quick introductory example is in order.

In the wrong hands, the tools covered here can be dangerous, introducing logic-defying bugs to your application that slither in the shadows during development only to rear their heads in production. But when honed and used properly, these tools allow your application to soar to new heights, squeezing never-before-seen levels of performance from your hardware.

Intro to Shared Memory

For this example you will build a very basic application that is able to communicate between two web workers. While this does require an initial bit of boilerplate using `postMessage()` and `onmessage`, subsequent updates won't rely on such functionality.

This shared memory example will work in a browser as well as in Node.js, though the setup work required is a little different for the two of them. For now, you'll build out an example that works in the browser, and a lot of description is provided. Later, once you're a little more familiar, you'll build out an example using Node.js.

Shared Memory in the Browser

To get started, create another directory to house this project in named *ch4-web-workers/*. Then, create an HTML file named *index.html*, and add the content from Example 4-1 to it.

Example 4-1. ch4-web-workers/index.html

```html
<html>
  <head>
    <title>Shared Memory Hello World</title>
    <script src="main.js"></script>
  </head>
</html>
```

Once you're done with that file you're ready for the more complicated part of the application. Create a file named *main.js* containing the content from Example 4-2.

Example 4-2. ch4-web-workers/main.js

```javascript
if (!crossOriginIsolated) { ❶
  throw new Error('Cannot use SharedArrayBuffer');
}

const worker = new Worker('worker.js');

const buffer = new SharedArrayBuffer(1024); ❷
const view = new Uint8Array(buffer); ❸

console.log('now', view[0]);

worker.postMessage(buffer);

setTimeout(() => {
  console.log('later', view[0]);
```

```
  console.log('prop', buffer.foo); ❹
}, 500);
```

❶ When `crossOriginIsolated` is true, then `SharedArrayBuffer` can be used.

❷ Instantiates a 1 KB buffer.

❸ A view into the buffer is created.

❹ A modified property is read.

This file is similar to one that you created before. In fact, it's still making use of a dedicated worker. But a few complexities have been added. The first new thing is the check for the `crossOriginIsolated` value, which is a global variable available in modern browsers. This value tells you if the JavaScript code currently being run is capable of, among other things, instantiating a `SharedArrayBuffer` instance.

For security reasons (related to the Spectre CPU attack), the `SharedArrayBuffer` object isn't always available for instantiation. In fact, a few years ago browsers disabled this functionality entirely. Now, both Chrome and Firefox support the object and require additional HTTP headers to be set when the document is served before it will allow a `SharedArrayBuffer` to be instantiated. Node.js doesn't have the same restrictions. Here are the required headers:

```
Cross-Origin-Opener-Policy: same-origin
Cross-Origin-Embedder-Policy: require-corp
```

The test server that you'll run automatically sets these headers. Any time you build a production-ready application that uses `SharedArrayBuffer` instances you'll need to remember to set these headers.

After a dedicated worker is instantiated, an instance of a `SharedArrayBuffer` is also instantiated. The argument that follows, 1,024 in this case, is the number of bytes allocated to the buffer. Unlike other arrays or buffer objects you might be familiar with, these buffers cannot shrink or grow in size after they've been created.[1]

A view to work with the buffer named `view` has also been created. Such views are covered extensively in "SharedArrayBuffer and TypedArrays" on page 79, but for now, think of them as a way to read from and write to a buffer.

This view into the buffer allows us to read from it using the array index syntax. In this case, we're able to inspect the 0th byte in the buffer by logging a call to `view[0]`. After that, the buffer instance is passed into the worker using the `worker.postMessage()`

---

1 This restriction may change in the future; see "In-Place Resizable and Growable ArrayBuffers" (*https://oreil.ly/im1CV*) for a proposal.

method. In this case the buffer is the only thing being passed in. However, a more complex object could have been passed in as well, with the buffer being one of the properties. Whereas the algorithm discussed in the Appendix mostly clobbers complex objects, instances of SharedArrayBuffer are an intentional exception.

Once the script is finished with the setup work, it schedules a function to run in 500 ms. This script prints the 0th byte of the buffer again and also attempts to print a property attached to the buffer named .foo. Note that this file otherwise does not have a worker.onmessage handler defined.

Now that you're finished with the main JavaScript file you're ready to create the worker. Make a file named *worker.js* and add the content from Example 4-3 to it.

Example 4-3. ch4-web-workers/worker.js

```
self.onmessage = ({data: buffer}) => {
  buffer.foo = 42; ❶
  const view = new Uint8Array(buffer);
  view[0] = 2; ❷
  console.log('updated in worker');
};
```

❶ A property on the buffer object is written.

❷ The 0th index is set to the number 2.

This file attaches a handler for the onmessage event, which is run after the .postMessage() method in *main.js* is fired. Once called, the buffer argument is grabbed. The first thing that happens in the handler is that a .foo property is attached to the SharedArrayBuffer instance. Next, another view is created for the buffer. After that the buffer is updated through the view. Once that's done, a message is printed so that you can see what has happened.

Now that your files are complete, you're ready to run your new application. Open up a terminal window and run the following command. It's a little different than the serve commands you ran before because it needs to provide the security headers:

```
$ npx MultithreadedJSBook/serve .
```

As before, open the link displayed in your terminal. Next, open the web inspector and visit the Console tab. You might not see any output; if so, refresh the page to execute the code again. You should see logs printed from the application. An example of the output has been reproduced in Table 4-1.

Table 4-1. Example console output

Log	Location
now 0	main.js:10:9
updated in worker	worker.js:5:11
later 2	main.js:15:11
prop undefined	main.js:16:11

The first printed line is the initial value of the buffer as seen in *main.js*. In this case the value is 0. Next, the code in *worker.js* is run, though the timing of this is mostly indeterminate. About half a second later, the value as perceived in *main.js* is printed again, and the value is now set to 2. Again, notice that other than the initial setup work, no message passing happened between the thread running the *main.js* file and the thread running the *worker.js* file.

> This is a very simple example that, while it works, is not how you would normally write multithreaded code. There is no guarantee that the value updated in *worker.js* would be visible in *main.js*. For example, a clever JavaScript engine could treat the value as a constant, though you'd be hard-pressed to find a browser where this doesn't happen.

After the buffer value is printed, the `.foo` property is also printed and a value of `undefined` is displayed. Why might this be? Well, while it's true that a reference to the memory location that stores the binary data contained in the buffer has been shared between the two JavaScript environments, the actual object itself has not been shared. If it had been, this would violate the constraint of the structured clone algorithm wherein object references cannot be shared between threads.

Shared Memory in Node.js

The Node.js equivalent of this application is mostly similar; however, the `Worker` global provided by browsers isn't available, and the worker thread won't make use of `self.onmessage`. Instead, the worker threads module must be required to gain access to this functionality. Since Node.js isn't a browser the *index.html* file isn't applicable.

To create a Node.js equivalent, you'll only need two files, which can be put in the same *ch4-web-workers/* folder you've been using. First, create a *main-node.js* script, and add the content from Example 4-4 to it.

Example 4-4. ch4-web-workers/main-node.js

```
#!/usr/bin/env node

const { Worker } = require('worker_threads');
const worker = new Worker(__dirname + '/worker-node.js');

const buffer = new SharedArrayBuffer(1024);
const view = new Uint8Array(buffer);

console.log('now', view[0]);

worker.postMessage(buffer);

setTimeout(() => {
  console.log('later', view[0]);
  console.log('prop', buffer.foo);
  worker.unref();
}, 500);
```

The code is a little different, but it should feel mostly familiar. Because the `Worker` global isn't available, it is instead accessed by pulling the `.Worker` property from the required `worker_threads` module. When instantiating the worker a more explicit path to the worker must be provided than what is accepted by browsers. In this case the path *./worker-node.js* was required, even though browsers are fine with just *worker.js*. Other than that, the main JavaScript file for this Node.js example is mostly unchanged when compared to the browser equivalent. The final `worker.unref()` call was added to prevent the worker from keeping the process running forever.

Next, create a file named *worker-node.js*, which will contain the Node.js equivalent of the browser worker. Add the content from Example 4-5 to this file.

Example 4-5. ch4-web-workers/worker-node.js

```
const { parentPort } = require('worker_threads');

parentPort.on('message', (buffer) => {
  buffer.foo = 42;
  const view = new Uint8Array(buffer);
  view[0] = 2;
  console.log('updated in worker');
});
```

In this case the `self.onmessage` value isn't available to the worker. Instead, the `worker_threads` module is required again, and the `.parentPort` property from the module is used. This is used to represent a connection to the port from the calling JavaScript environment.

The `.onmessage` handler can be assigned to the `parentPort` object, and the method `.on('message', cb)` can be called. If using both, they'll be called in the order that they were used. The callback function for the `message` event receives the object being passed in (`buffer` in this case) directly as an argument, while the `onmessage` handler provides a `MessageEvent` instance with a `.data` property containing `buffer`. Which approach you use mostly depends on personal preference.

Other than that the code is exactly the same between Node.js and the browser, the same applicable globals like `SharedArrayBuffer` are still available, and they still work the same for the sake of this example.

Now that these files are complete, you can run them using this command:

```
$ node main-node.js
```

The output from this command should be equivalent to the output in Table 4-1 as displayed in the browser. Again, the same structured clone algorithm allows instances of `SharedArrayBuffer` to be passed along, but only the underlying binary buffer data, not a direct reference to the object itself.

SharedArrayBuffer and TypedArrays

Traditionally the JavaScript language didn't really support interaction with binary data. Sure, there were strings, but they really abstracted the underlying data storage mechanism. There were also arrays, but those can contain values of any type and aren't appropriate for representing binary buffers. For many years that was sort of "good enough," especially before the advent of Node.js and the popularity of running JavaScript outside of a web page context took off.

The Node.js runtime is, among other things, capable of reading and writing to the filesystem, streaming data to and from the network, and so on. Such interactions are not only limited to ASCII-based text files but can also include piping binary data as well. Since there wasn't a convenient buffer data structure available, the authors created their own. Thus, the Node.js `Buffer` was born.

As the boundaries of the JavaScript language itself were pushed, so too grew the APIs and the capabilities of the language to interact with the world outside of the browser window. Eventually the `ArrayBuffer` object and later the `SharedArrayBuffer` object were created and are now a core part of the language. Most likely, if Node.js were created today, it would not have created its own `Buffer` implementation.

Instances of `ArrayBuffer` and `SharedArrayBuffer` represent a buffer of binary data that is of fixed length and cannot be resized. While the two are quite similar, it is the latter that will be the focus of this section because it allows applications to share memory across threads. Binary data, while ubiquitous and a first-class concept in many traditional programming languages like C, can be easy to misunderstand, especially for developers using high-level languages such as JavaScript.

Just in case you haven't had experience with it, *binary* is a system of counting that is 2 based, which at the lowest level is represented as 1s and 0s. Each of these numbers is referred to as a *bit*. *Decimal*, the system humans mostly use for counting, is 10 based and is represented with numerals from 0 to 9. A combination of 8 bits is referred to as a byte and is often the smallest addressable value in memory since it's usually easier to deal with than individual bits. Basically, this means CPUs (and programmers) work with bytes instead of individual bits.

These bytes are often represented as two *hexadecimal* characters, which is a 16 based system of counting using the numerals 0–9 and the letters A–F. In fact, when you log an instance of an `ArrayBuffer` using Node.js, the resulting output displays the value of the buffer using hexadecimal.

Given an arbitrary set of bytes that is stored on disk, or even in a computer's memory, it's a little ambiguous what the data means. For example, what might the hexadecimal value `0x54` (the `0x` prefix in JavaScript means the value is in hexadecimal) represent? Well, if it's part of a string, it might mean the capital letter *T*. However, if it represents an integer, it might mean the decimal number 84. It might even refer to a memory location, part of a pixel in a JPEG image, or any other number of things. The context here is very important. That same number, represented in binary, looks like `0b01010100` (the `0b` prefix represents binary).

Keeping this ambiguity in mind, it's also important to mention that the contents of an `ArrayBuffer` (and `SharedArrayBuffer`) can't be directly modified. Instead, a "view" into the buffer must first be created. Also, unlike other languages which might provide access to abandoned memory, when an `ArrayBuffer` in JavaScript is instantiated the contents of the buffer are initialized to 0. Considering these buffer objects only store numeric data, they truly are a very elementary tool for data storage, one that more complicated systems are often built upon.

Both `ArrayBuffer` and `SharedArrayBuffer` inherit from `Object` and come with those associated methods. Other than that, they come with two properties. The first is the read-only value `.byteLength`, representing the byte length of the buffer, and the second is the `.slice(begin, end)` method, which returns a copy of the buffer depending on the range that is provided.

The `begin` value of `.slice()` is inclusive, while the `end` value is exclusive, and is notably different than, say, `String#substr(begin, length)`, where the second parameter is a length. If the `begin` value is omitted, it defaults to the first element, and if the `end` value is omitted, it defaults to the last element. Negative numbers represent values from the end of the buffer.

Here's an example of some basic interaction with an `ArrayBuffer`:

```
const ab = new ArrayBuffer(8);
const view = new Uint8Array(ab)
for (i = 0; i < 8; i++) view[i] = i;
console.log(view);
// Uint8Array(8) [
//   0, 1, 2, 3,
//   4, 5, 6, 7
// ]
ab.byteLength; // 8
ab.slice(); // 0, 1, 2, 3, 4, 5, 6, 7
ab.slice(4, 6); // 4, 5
ab.slice(-3, -2); // 5
```

Different JavaScript environments display the contents of an `ArrayBuffer` instance differently. Node.js displays a list of hexadecimal pairs as if the data were going to be viewed as a `Uint8Array`. Chrome v88 displays an expandable object with several different views. Firefox, however, won't display the data, and will need to first be passed through a view.

The term *view* has been mentioned in a few places, and now is a good time to define it. Due to the ambiguity of what binary data can mean, we need to use a view to read and write to the underlying buffer. There are several of these views available in JavaScript. Each of these views extends from a base class called `TypedArray`. This class can't be instantiated directly and isn't available as a global, but it can be accessed by grabbing the `.prototype` property from an instantiated child class.

Table 4-2 contains a list of the view classes that extend from `TypedArray`.

Table 4-2. Classes that extend `TypedArray`

Class	Bytes	Minimum Value	Maximum Value
Int8Array	1	−128	127
Uint8Array	1	0	255
Uint8ClampedArray	1	0	255
Int16Array	2	−32,768	32,767
Uint16Array	2	0	65,535
Int32Array	4	−2,147,483,648	2,147,483,647
Uint32Array	4	0	4294967295
Float32Array	4	1.4012984643e−45	3.4028235e38
Float64Array	8	5e−324	1.7976931348623157e308
BigInt64Array	8	−9,223,372,036,854,775,808	9,223,372,036,854,775,807
BigUint64Array	8	0	18,446,744,073,709,551,615

The Class column is the name of the class that is available for instantiation. These classes are globals and are accessible in any modern JavaScript engine. The Bytes column is the number of bytes that are used to represent each individual element in the view. The Minimum Value and Maximum Value columns display the valid numeric ranges that can be used to represent an element in the buffer.

When creating one of these views, the `ArrayBuffer` instance is passed into the constructor of the view. The buffer byte length must be a multiple of the element byte length used by the particular view that it's being passed into. For example, if an `ArrayBuffer` composed of 6 bytes were created, it is acceptable to pass that into an `Int16Array` (byte length of 2) because this will represent three `Int16` elements. However, the same 6-byte buffer cannot be passed into an `Int32Array` because it would represent one and a half elements, which isn't valid.

The names of these views might be familiar if you've programmed with lower-level languages such as C or Rust.

The `U` prefix to half of these classes refers to unsigned, which means that only positive numbers may be represented. Classes without the `U` prefix are signed and so negative and positive numbers may be represented, though with only half the maximum value. This is because a signed number uses the first bit to represent the "sign," conveying if the number is positive or negative.

The numeric range limitations come from the amount of data that can be stored in a single byte to uniquely identify a number. Much like with decimal, numbers are counted from zero on up to the base, and then roll over to a number on the left. So, for a `Uint8` number, or an "unsigned integer represented by 8 bits," the maximum value (`0b11111111`) is equal to 255.

JavaScript doesn't have an integer data type, only its `Number` type, which is an implementation of the IEEE 754 floating-point number (*https://oreil.ly/gOSK8*). It is equivalent to the `Float64` data type. Otherwise, any time a JavaScript `Number` is written to one of these views, some sort of conversion process needs to happen.

When a value is written to `Float64Array`, it can be left mostly as the same. The minimum allowed value is the same as `Number.MIN_VALUE`, while the maximum is `Number.MAX_VALUE`. When a value is written to a `Float32Array`, not only are the minimum and maximum value ranges reduced but the decimal precision will be truncated as well.

As an example of this, consider the following code:

```
const buffer = new ArrayBuffer(16);

const view64 = new Float64Array(buffer);
view64[0] = 1.1234567890123456789; // bytes 0 - 7
console.log(view64[0]); // 1.1234567890123457
```

```
const view32 = new Float32Array(buffer);
view32[2] = 1.1234567890123456789; // bytes 8 - 11
console.log(view32[2]); // 1.1234568357467651
```

In this case, the decimal precision for the float64 number is accurate to the 15th decimal, while the precision for the float32 number is only accurate to the 6th decimal.

This code exemplifies another thing of interest. In this case, there is a single Array Buffer instance named buffer, and yet there are two different TypedArray instances that point to this buffer data. Can you think of what's weird with this? Figure 4-1 might give you a hint.

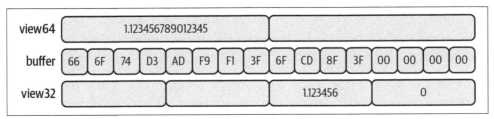

Figure 4-1. Single ArrayBuffer and multiple TypeArray views

What do you think will be returned if you were to read either view64[1], view32[0], or view32[1]? In this case, a truncated version of the memory used to store data of one type will be combined, or split, to represent data of another type. The values returned are interpreted in the wrong way and are nonsensical, though they should be deterministic and consistent.

When numeric values that are outside of the range of the supported TypedArray for nonfloats are written, they need to go through some sort of conversion process to fit the target data type. First, the number must be converted into an integer, as if it were passed into Math.trunc(). If the value falls outside of the acceptable range, then it wraps around and resets at 0 as if using the modulus (%) operator. Here are some examples of this happening with a Uint8Array (which is a TypedArray with a max element value of 255):

```
const buffer = new ArrayBuffer(8);
const view = new Uint8Array(buffer);
view[0] = 255;     view[1] = 256;
view[2] = 257;     view[3] = -1;
view[4] = 1.1;     view[5] = 1.999;
view[6] = -1.1;    view[7] = -1.9;
console.log(view);
```

Table 4-3 contains a list of the values output on the second line, with their correlating values on the first line.

Table 4-3. TypedArray conversions

Input	255	256	257	−1	1.1	1.999	−1.1	−1.9
Output	255	0	1	255	1	1	255	255

This behavior is a little different for `Uint8ClampedArray`. When a negative value is written, it is converted into 0. When a value greater than 255 is written, it's converted into 255. When a noninteger value is provided, it's instead passed to `Math.round()`. Depending on your use case, it may make more sense to use this view.

Finally, the `BigInt64Array` and `BigUint64Array` entries also deserve some special attention. Unlike the other `TypedArray` views, which work with the `Number` type, these two variants work with the `BigInt` type (1 is a `Number` while 1n is a `BigInt`). This is because the numeric values that can be represented using 64 bytes fall out of the range of the numbers than can be represented using JavaScript's `Number`. For that reason, setting a value with these views must be done with a `BigInt`, and the values retrieved will also be of type `BigInt`.

In general, using multiple `TypedArray` views, especially those of different sizes, to look into the same buffer instance is a dangerous thing and should be avoided when possible. You might find that you accidentally clobber some data when performing different operations. It is possible to pass more than one `SharedArrayBuffer` between threads, so if you find yourself needing to mix types, then you might benefit from having more than one buffer.

Now that you're familiar with the basics of `ArrayBuffer` and `SharedArrayBuffer` you're ready to interact with them using a more complex API.

Atomic Methods for Data Manipulation

Atomicity is a term that you might have heard before, particularly when it comes to databases, where it's the first word in the acronym ACID (atomicity, consistency, isolation, durability). Essentially, if an operation is *atomic*, it means that while the overall operation may be composed of multiple smaller steps, the overall operation is guaranteed to either entirely succeed or entirely fail. For example, a single query sent to a database is going to be atomic, but three separate queries aren't atomic.

Then again, if those three queries are wrapped in a database transaction, then the whole lot becomes atomic; either all three queries run successfully, or none run successfully. It's also important that the operations are executed in a particular order, assuming they manipulate the same state or otherwise have any side effects than can affect each other. The *isolation* part means that other operations can't run in the middle; for example, a read can't occur when only some of the operations have been applied.

Atomic operations are very important in computing, especially when it comes to distributed computing. Databases, which may have many client connections, need to support atomic operations. Distributed systems, where many nodes on a network communicate, also need to support atomic operations. Extrapolating that idea a little, even within a single computer where data access is shared across multiple threads, atomicity is important.

JavaScript provides a global object named `Atomics` with several static methods available on it. This global follows the same pattern as the familiar `Math` global. In either case you can't use the `new` operator to create a new instance, and the available methods are stateless, not affecting the global itself. Instead, with `Atomics`, they're used by passing in a reference to the data that is to be modified.

The rest of this section lists all but three of the methods that are available on the `Atomics` object. The remaining methods are covered in "Atomic Methods for Coordination" on page 97. With the exception of `Atomics.isLockFree()`, all of these methods accept a `TypedArray` instance as the first argument and the index to act upon as the second argument.

Atomics.add()

```
old = Atomics.add(typedArray, index, value)
```

This method adds the provided `value` to the existing value in a `typedArray` that is located at `index`. The old value is returned. Here's what the nonatomic version might look like:

```
const old = typedArray[index];
typedArray[index] = old + value;
return old;
```

Atomics.and()

```
old = Atomics.and(typedArray, index, value)
```

This method performs a bitwise and using `value` with the existing value in `typedArray` located at `index`. The old value is returned. Here's what the nonatomic version might look like:

```
const old = typedArray[index];
typedArray[index] = old & value;
return old;
```

Atomics.compareExchange()

```
old = Atomics.compareExchange(typedArray, index, oldExpectedValue, value)
```

This method checks `typedArray` to see if the value `oldExpectedValue` is located at `index`. If it is, then the value is replaced with `value`. If not, then nothing happens. The old value is always returned, so you can tell if the exchange succeeded if `oldExpected Value === old`. Here's what the nonatomic version might look like:

```
const old = typedArray[index];
if (old === oldExpectedValue) {
  typedArray[index] = value;
}
return old;
```

Atomics.exchange()

```
old = Atomics.exchange(typedArray, index, value)
```

This method sets the value in `typedArray` located at `index` to `value`. The old value is returned. Here's what the nonatomic version might look like:

```
const old = typedArray[index];
typedArray[index] = value;
return old;
```

Atomics.isLockFree()

```
free = Atomics.isLockFree(size)
```

This method returns a `true` if `size` is a value that appears as the `BYTES_PER_ELEMENT` for any of the `TypedArray` subclasses (usually 1, 2, 4, 8), and a `false` if otherwise.[2] If `true`, then using the `Atomics` methods will be quite fast using the current system's hardware. If `false`, then the application might want to use a manual locking mechanism, like what is covered in "Mutex: A Basic Lock" on page 131, especially if performance is the main concern.

Atomics.load()

```
value = Atomics.load(typedArray, index)
```

This method returns the value in `typedArray` located at `index`. Here's what the nonatomic version might look like:

---

2 If running JavaScript on rare hardware, it is possible that this method may return a `false` for 1, 2, or 8. That said, 4 will always return `true`.

```
const old = typedArray[index];
return old;
```

Atomics.or()

```
old = Atomics.or(typedArray, index, value)
```

This method performs a bitwise or using value with the existing value in typedArray located at index. The old value is returned. Here's what the nonatomic version might look like:

```
const old = typedArray[index];
typedArray[index] = old | value;
return old;
```

Atomics.store()

```
value = Atomics.store(typedArray, index, value)
```

This method stores the provided value in typedArray located at index. The value that was passed in is then returned. Here's what the nonatomic version might look like:

```
typedArray[index] = value;
return value;
```

Atomics.sub()

```
old = Atomics.sub(typedArray, index, value)
```

This method subtracts the provided value from the existing value in typedArray that is located at index. The old value is returned. Here's what the nonatomic version might look like:

```
const old = typedArray[index];
typedArray[index] = old - value;
return old;
```

Atomics.xor()

```
old = Atomics.xor(typedArray, index, value)
```

This method performs a bitwise xor using value with the existing value in typedArray located at index. The old value is returned. Here's what the nonatomic version might look like:

```
const old = typedArray[index];
typedArray[index] = old ^ value;
return old;
```

Atomicity Concerns

The methods covered in "Atomic Methods for Data Manipulation" on page 84 are each guaranteed to execute atomically. For example, consider the `Atomics.compareEx change()` method. This method takes an `oldExpectedValue` and a new `value`, replacing the existing value only if it equals `oldExpectedValue` with the new `value`. While this operation would take several individual statements to represent with JavaScript, it's guaranteed that the overall operation will always execute entirely.

To illustrate this, imagine you have a `Uint8Array` named `typedArray`, and the 0th element is set to 7. Then, imagine that multiple threads have access to that same `typedArray`, and each of them executes some variant of the following line of code:

```
let old1 = Atomics.compareExchange(typedArray, 0, 7, 1); // Thread #1
let old2 = Atomics.compareExchange(typedArray, 0, 7, 2); // Thread #2
```

It's entirely nondeterministic the order that these three methods are called in, or even the timing of their calls. In fact, they could be called simultaneously! However, with the atomicity guarantee of the `Atomics` object, it's guaranteed that exactly one of the threads will have the initial 7 value returned, while the other thread will get the updated value of 1 or 2 returned. A timeline of how these operations work can be seen in Figure 4-2, with the `CEX(oldExpectedValue, value)` being a shorthand for `Atomics.compareExchange()`.

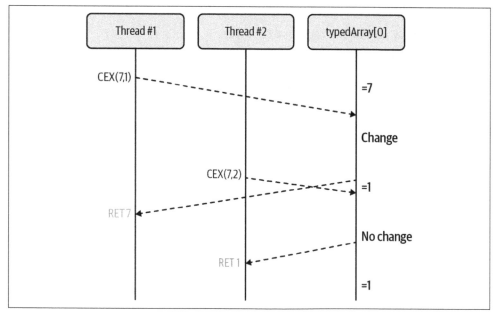

Figure 4-2. Atomic form of `Atomics.compareExchange()`

On the other hand, if you're using the nonatomic equivalent of compareExchange(), such as reading and writing to typedArray[0] directly, it is entirely possible that the program will accidentally clobber a value. In this case both threads read the existing value at about the same time, then they both see that the original value is present, then they both write at about the same time. Here is an annotated version of the nonatomic compareExchange() code again:

```
const old = typedArray[0]; // GET()
if (old === oldExpectedValue) {
  typedArray[0] = value;    // SET(value)
}
```

This code performs multiple interactions with shared data, notably the line where the data is retrieved (labeled as GET()) and later where the data is later set (labeled as SET(value)). For this code to function properly it would need a guarantee that other threads aren't able to read or write to the value while the code is running. This guarantees that only one thread gets exclusive access to shared resources is called a *critical section*.

Figure 4-3 shows a timeline of how this code might run, as is, without the exclusive access guarantees.

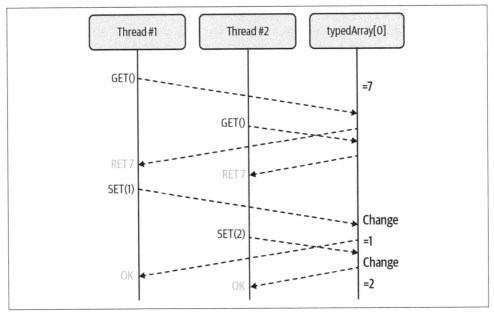

Figure 4-3. Nonatomic form of Atomics.compareExchange()

In this case both threads think they have successfully set the value, but the desired outcome only persists for the second thread. This class of bug is referred to as a *race condition*, where two or more threads are racing against each other to perform some action.[3] The worst thing about these bugs is that they don't happen consistently, are notoriously hard to reproduce, and may only happen in one environment, such as a production server, and not another environment, like your development laptop.

To benefit from the atomic properties of the `Atomics` object when interacting with an array buffer, you'll need to take care when mixing `Atomics` calls with direct array buffer access. If one thread of your application is using the `compareExchange()` method, and another thread is directly reading and writing to the same buffer location, then the safety mechanisms will have been defeated and your application will have nondeterministic behavior. Essentially, when using `Atomics` calls, there's an implicit lock in place to make interactions convenient.

Sadly, not all of the operations you'll need to perform with shared memory can be represented using the `Atomics` methods. When that happens you'll need to come up with a more manual locking mechanism, allowing you to read and write freely and preventing other threads from doing so. This concept is covered later in "Mutex: A Basic Lock" on page 131.

Return Values Ignore Conversion

One caveat concerning the `Atomics` methods is that the returned values aren't necessarily aware of the conversion that the particular `TypedArray` will go through, but instead consider the value *before* going through the conversion. For example, consider the following situation where a value is stored that is larger than what can be represented by the given view:

```
const buffer = new SharedArrayBuffer(1);
const view = new Uint8Array(buffer);
const ret = Atomics.store(view, 0, 999);
console.log(ret); // 999
console.log(view[0]); // 231
```

This code creates a buffer and then a `Uint8Array` view into that array. It then uses `Atomics.store()` to store the value 999 using the view. The return value from the `Atomics.store()` call is the value that was passed in, 999, even though the value that was actually stored in the underlying buffer is the value 231 (999 is greater than the maximum supported 255). You will need to keep this limitation in mind when building your applications. To stay on the safe side, you should craft your application to not rely on this data conversion and only write values that are within range.

---

3 It's possible, with the way code is compiled, ordered, and executed, that a racy program can fail in a way that can't be explained by this diagram of interleaving steps. When this happens you may end up with a value that defies all expectations.

Data Serialization

Buffers are extremely powerful tools. That said, working with them from an entirely numeric point of view can start to get a little difficult. Sometimes you'll need to store things that represent nonnumeric data using a buffer. When this happens you'll need to serialize that data in some manner before writing it to the buffer, and you'll later need to deserialize it when reading from the buffer.

Depending on the type of data that you'd like to represent, there will be different tools that you can use to serialize it. Some tools will work for different situations, but each comes with different trade-offs with regard to storage size and serialization performance.

Booleans

Booleans are easy to represent because they take a single bit to store the data, and a bit is less than a byte. So you can then create one of the smallest views, such as a `Uint8Array`, then point it at an `ArrayBuffer` with a byte length of 1, and be set. Of course, the interesting thing here is that you can then store up to eight of these booleans using a single byte. In fact, if you're dealing with a ton of boolean values, you might be able to outperform the JavaScript engine by storing large numbers of them in a buffer since there is additional metadata overhead for each boolean instance. Figure 4-4 shows a list of booleans represented as a byte.

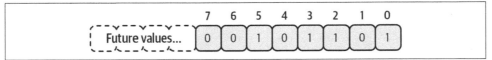

Figure 4-4. Boolean values stored in a byte

When storing data in individual bits like this, it's best to start with the least significant bit, e.g., the bit farthest to the right labeled 0, then move on to more significant bits if you find yourself adding more booleans to the byte that you're storing them in. The reason for this is simple: as the number of booleans you need to store grows, so too will the size of the buffer, and existing bit locations should remain correct. While the buffer itself can't grow dynamically, newer releases of your application might need to instantiate large buffers.

If the buffer that stores the booleans is today 1 byte, and tomorrow 2 bytes, by using the least significant digits first the decimal representation of the data will remain either a 0 or a 1. However, if the most significant digit were used, then today the value might be 0 and 128, while tomorrow it might be 32,768 and 0. This could potentially cause issues if you're persisting these values somewhere and using them between releases.

The following is an example of how to store and retrieve these boolean values so that they're backed in an `ArrayBuffer`:

```
const buffer = new ArrayBuffer(1);
const view = new Uint8Array(buffer);
function setBool(slot, value) {
  view[0] = (view[0] & ~(1 << slot)) | ((value|0) << slot);
}
function getBool(slot) {
  return !((view[0] & (1 << slot)) === 0);
}
```

This code creates a one-byte buffer (`0b00000000` in binary) then creates a view into the buffer. To set the value in the least significant digit in the `ArrayBuffer` to true, you would use the call `setBool(0, true)`. To set the second least significant digit to false, you would call `setBool(1, false)`. To retrieve the values stored at the third least significant digit, you would then call `getBool(2)`.

The `setBool()` function works by taking the boolean `value` and converting it into an integer (`value|0` converts `false` to 0 and `true` to 1). Then it "shifts the value left" by adding zeros to the right based on which `slot` to store it in (`0b1<<0` stays `0b1`, `0b1<<1` becomes `0b10`, etc.). It also takes the number 1 and shifts it based on the `slot` (so `0b1000` if the `slot` is 3), then inverts the bits (using `~`), and gets a new value by AND-ing (`&`) the existing value with this new value (`view[0] & ~(1 << slot)`). Finally, the modified old value and the new shifted values are OR-ed together (`|`) and assigned to `view[0]`. Basically, it reads the existing bits, replaces the appropriate bit, and writes the bits back.

The `getBool()` function works by taking the number 1, shifting it based on the slot, then using `&` to compare it to the existing value. The shifted value (on the right of `&`) only contains a single 1 and seven 0s. The AND-ing between this modified value and the existing value returns either a number representing the value of the shifted slot, assuming the value at the `slot` position located at `view[0]` was truthy; otherwise, it returns 0. This value is then checked to see if it is exactly equal to 0 (`===0`), and the result of that is negated (`!`). Basically, it returns the value of the bit at `slot`.

This code has some shortcomings and shouldn't necessarily be used in production. For example, it isn't meant for working with buffers that are larger than a single byte, and you'll encounter undefined behavior when reading or writing to entries past 7. A production-ready version would consider the size of storage and do bounds checking, but that's an exercise left to the reader.

Strings

Strings aren't as easy to encode as they may seem at first glance. It's easy to assume that each character in a string can be represented using a single byte, and that the .length property of a string is sufficient to choose the size of a buffer to store it in. While this may seem to work sometimes, particularly with simple strings, you'll soon encounter errors when dealing with more complex data.

The reason this will work with simple strings is that data represented using ASCII does allow a single character to fit into a single byte. In fact, in the C programming language, the data storage type that represents a single byte of data is referred to as a char.

There are many ways to encode individual characters using strings. With ASCII the entire range of characters can be represented with a byte, but in a world of many cultures, languages, and emojis, it's absolutely impossible to represent all these characters in such a manner. Instead, we use encoding systems where a variable number of bytes can be used to represent a single character. Internally, JavaScript engines use a variety of encoding formats to represent strings depending on the situation, and the complexity of this is hidden from our applications. One possible internal format is UTF-16, which uses 2 or 4 bytes to represent a character, or even up to 14 bytes to represent certain emojis. A more universal standard is UTF-8, which uses 1 to 4 bytes of storage per character and is backwards compatible with ASCII.

The following is an example of what happens when a string is iterated using its .length property and the resulting values are mapped to a Uint8Array instance:

```
// Warning: Antipattern!
function stringToArrayBuffer(str) {
  const buffer = new ArrayBuffer(str.length);
  const view = new Uint8Array(buffer);
  for (let i = 0; i < str.length; i++) {
    view[i] = str.charCodeAt(i);
  }
  return view;
}

stringToArrayBuffer('foo'); // Uint8Array(3) [ 102, 111, 111 ]
stringToArrayBuffer('€');   // Uint8Array(1) [ 172 ]
```

In this case storing the basic string foo is fine. However, the € character, which is really represented by the value 8,364, is greater than the maximum 255 value supported by Uint8Array and has accordingly been truncated to 172. Converting that number back into a character gives the wrong value.

An API is available to modern JavaScript for encoding and decoding strings directly to `ArrayBuffer` instances. This API is provided by the globals `TextEncoder` and `Text Decoder`, both of which are constructors and are globally available in modern JavaScript environments including browsers and Node.js. These APIs encode and decode using the UTF-8 encoding due to its ubiquity.

Here's an example of how to safely encode strings into the UTF-8 encoding using this API:

```
const enc = new TextEncoder();
enc.encode('foo'); // Uint8Array(3) [ 102, 111, 111 ]
enc.encode('€');   // Uint8Array(3) [ 226, 130, 172 ]
```

And here's how to decode such values:

```
const ab = new ArrayBuffer(3);
const view = new Uint8Array(ab);
view[0] = 226; view[1] = 130; view[2] = 172;
const dec = new TextDecoder();
dec.decode(view); // '€'
dec.decode(ab);   // '€'
```

Notice that `TextDecoder#decode()` works with either the `Uint8Array` view, or with the underlying `ArrayBuffer` instance. This makes it convenient to decode data that you might get from a network call without the need to first wrap it in a view.

Objects

Considering that objects can already be represented as strings using JSON, you do have the option of taking an object that you'd like to make use of across two threads, serializing it into a JSON string, and writing that string to an array buffer using the same `TextEncoder` API that you worked with in the previous section. This can essentially be performed by running the following code:

```
const enc = new TextEncoder();
return enc.encode(JSON.stringify(obj));
```

JSON takes a JavaScript object and converts it into a string representation. When this happens, there are many redundancies in the output format. If you wanted to reduce the size of a payload even more, you could make use of a format like MessagePack (*https://msgpack.org*), which is able to reduce the size of a serialized object even more by representing object metadata using binary data. This makes tools like Message-Pack not necessarily a good fit in situations where plain text is appropriate, like an email, but in situations where binary buffers are passed around it might not be as bad. The `msgpack5` npm package is a browser and Node.js compatible package for doing just that.

That said, the performance trade-offs when communicating between threads is not usually due to the size of the payload being transferred, but is more than likely due to the cost of serializing and deserializing payloads. For that reason it's usually better to pass simpler data representations between threads. Even when it comes to passing objects between threads, you might find that the structured clone algorithm, combined with the .onmessage and .postMessage methods, is going to be faster and safer than serializing objects and writing them to buffers.

If you do find yourself building an application that serializes and deserializes objects and writes them to a SharedArrayBuffer, you might want to reconsider some of the architecture of the application. You're almost always better off finding a way to take objects that you're passing around, serializing them using lower-level types, and passing those along instead.

## CHAPTER 5

Advanced Shared Memory

Chapter 4 looked at using the `SharedArrayBuffer` object to read and write directly to a collection of shared data from across separate threads. But doing so is risky business, allowing one thread to clobber data that was written by another thread. However, thanks to the `Atomics` object, you are able to perform very basic operations with that data in a way that prevents data from being clobbered.

Although the basic operations provided by `Atomics` are convenient, you will often find yourself needing to perform more complex interactions with that data. For example, once you've serialized data as described in "Data Serialization" on page 91, like a 1 kilobyte string, you'll then need to write that data to the `SharedArrayBuffer` instance, and none of the existing `Atomics` methods will allow you to set the entire value all at once.

This chapter covers additional functionality for coordinating reads and writes to shared data across threads for situations when the previously covered `Atomics` methods just aren't enough.

Atomic Methods for Coordination

These methods are a little different than the ones that were already covered in "Atomic Methods for Data Manipulation" on page 84. Specifically, the methods previously covered each work with a `TypedArray` of any kind and may operate on both `SharedArrayBuffer` and `ArrayBuffer` instances. However, the methods listed here will only work with `Int32Array` and `BigInt64Array` instances, and they only make sense when used with `SharedArrayBuffer` instances.

If you try to use these methods with the wrong type of `TypedArray`, you'll get one of these errors:

```
# Firefox v88
Uncaught TypeError: invalid array type for the operation

# Chrome v90 / Node.js v16
Uncaught TypeError: [object Int8Array] is not an int32 or BigInt64 typed array.
```

As far as prior art goes, these methods are modeled after a feature available in the Linux kernel called the *futex*, which is short for *fast userspace mutex*. *Mutex* itself is short for *mutual exclusion*, which is when a single thread of execution gets exclusive access to a particular piece of data. A mutex can also be referred to as a *lock*, where one thread locks access to the data, does its thing, and then unlocks access, allowing another thread to then touch the data. A futex is built on two basic operations, one being "wait" and the other being "wake."

Atomics.wait()

```
status = Atomics.wait(typedArray, index, value, timeout = Infinity)
```

This method first checks typedArray to see if the value at index is equal to value. If it is not, the function returns the value not-equal. If the value is equal, it will then freeze the thread for up to timeout milliseconds. If nothing happens during that time, the function returns the value timed-out. On the other hand, if another thread calls Atomics.notify() for that same index within the time period, the function then returns with a value of ok. Table 5-1 lists these return values.

Table 5-1. Return values from Atomics.wait()

Value	Meaning
not-equal	The provided value didn't equal the value present in the buffer.
timed-out	Another thread didn't call Atomics.notify() within the allotted timeout.
ok	Another thread did call Atomics.notify() in time.

You might be wondering why this method doesn't throw an error for the first two conditions and silently succeed instead of returning an ok. Because multithreaded programming is used for performance reasons, it stands to reason that calling these Atomics methods will be done in the *hotpaths* of an application, which are areas where the application spends the most time. It's less performant in JavaScript to instantiate Error objects and generate stack traces than to return a simple string, so the performance of this approach is pretty high. Another reason is that the not-equal case doesn't really represent an error case but that something you're waiting for has already happened.

This blocking behavior might be a little shocking at first. Locking an entire thread sounds a bit intense, and in many cases it is. Another example of what can cause an entire JavaScript thread to lock is the alert() function in a browser. When that function is called, the browser displays a dialog and nothing at all can run—not even any background tasks using the event loop—until the dialog is dismissed. The `Atomics.wait()` method similarly freezes the thread.

This behavior is so extreme, in fact, that the "main" thread—the default thread that is available when running JavaScript, outside of a web worker—is not allowed to call this method, at least in a browser. The reason is that locking the main thread would be such a poor user experience that the API authors didn't even want to allow it. If you do try to call this method in the main thread of a browser, you will get one of the following errors:

```
# Firefox
Uncaught TypeError: waiting is not allowed on this thread
```

```
# Chrome v90
Uncaught TypeError: Atomics.wait cannot be called in this context
```

Node.js, on the other hand, does allow `Atomics.wait()` to be called in the main thread. Since Node.js doesn't have a UI, this isn't necessarily a bad thing. Indeed, it can be useful when writing scripts where calling `fs.readFileSync()` is acceptable.

If you're a JavaScript developer who has ever worked at a company with mobile or desktop developers, you may have overheard them talk about "offloading work from the main thread" or "locking the main thread." These concerns, which have traditionally belonged to developers of native apps, will be enjoyed by us JavaScript engineers more and more as the language advances. With regards to browsers this issue is often referred to as *scroll jank*, which is when a CPU is too busy to draw the UI while scrolling.

Atomics.notify()

```
awaken = Atomics.notify(typedArray, index, count = Infinity)
```

The `Atomics.notify()`[1] method attempts to awaken other threads that have called `Atomics.wait()` on the same `typedArray` and at the same `index`. If any other threads are currently frozen, then they will wake up. Multiple threads can be frozen at the same time, each waiting to be notified. The `count` value then determines how many of them to awaken. The `count` value defaults to `Infinity`, meaning that every thread will be awakened. However, if you have four threads waiting and set the value to three, then all but one of them will be woken up. "Timing and Nondeterminism" on page 100 examines the order of these waking threads.

---

1 `Atomics.notify()` was originally going to be called `Atomics.wake()` like its Linux futex equivalent but was later renamed to prevent visual confusion between "wake" and "wait" methods.

The return value is the number of threads that have been awoken once the method is complete. If you were to pass in a `TypedArray` instance that points to a nonshared `ArrayBuffer` instance, this will always return a 0. If no threads happen to be listening at the time it will also return a 0. Because this method doesn't block the thread, it can always be called from a main JavaScript thread.

Atomics.waitAsync()

```
promise = Atomics.waitAsync(typedArray, index, value, timeout = Infinity)
```

This is essentially a promise-based version of `Atomics.wait()` and is the latest addition to the `Atomics` family. As of this writing it is available in Node.js v16 and Chrome v87 but not yet available in Firefox or Safari.

This method is essentially a less-performant, nonblocking version of `Atomics.wait()` that returns a promise which resolves the status of the wait operation. Due to the loss of performance (a resolving promise is going to have more overhead than pausing a thread and returning a string), it isn't necessarily as useful for the hotpath of a CPU-heavy algorithm. On the other hand, it can be useful in situations where a lock change is more convenient to signal another thread than to perform message-passing operations via `postMessage()`. Because this method doesn't block the thread, it can be used in the main thread of an application.

One of the driving factors for adding this method is so that code compiled using Emscripten (covered in "Compiling C Programs to WebAssembly with Emscripten" on page 159) that makes use of threading is allowed to execute in the main thread and not just in worker threads.

Timing and Nondeterminism

In order for an application to be correct it usually needs to behave in a deterministic fashion. The `Atomics.notify()` function accepts an argument `count` that contains the number of threads to wake up. The glaring question in this situation is which threads get woken up and in which order?

Example of Nondeterminism

Threads are woken up in *FIFO* (first in, first out) order, meaning the first thread that called `Atomics.wait()` is the first to be woken up, the second to call is the second to be woken up, and so on. Measuring this can be difficult, however, because log messages printed from different workers aren't guaranteed to be displayed in the terminal in the true order that they were executed in. Ideally, you should build your application in such a way that it continues to work fine regardless of the order in which threads have been awoken.

To test this for yourself, you can create a new application. First, create a new directory named *ch5-notify-order/*. In it, start off by creating another basic *index.html* file using the content from Example 5-1.

Example 5-1. ch5-notify-order/index.html

```html
<html>
  <head>
    <title>Shared Memory for Coordination</title>
    <script src="main.js"></script>
  </head>
</html>
```

Next, create another *main.js* file, containing the content from Example 5-2.

Example 5-2. ch5-notify-order/main.js

```javascript
if (!crossOriginIsolated) throw new Error('Cannot use SharedArrayBuffer');

const buffer = new SharedArrayBuffer(4);
const view = new Int32Array(buffer);

for (let i = 0; i < 4; i++) { ❶
  const worker = new Worker('worker.js');
  worker.postMessage({buffer, name: i});
}

setTimeout(() => {
  Atomics.notify(view, 0, 3); ❷
}, 500); ❸
```

❶ Four dedicated workers are instantiated.

❷ The shared buffer is notified at index 0.

❸ The notification is sent at half a second.

This file first creates a 4-byte buffer, which is the smallest buffer that can support the needed `Int32Array` view. Next, it creates four different dedicated workers using a `for` loop. For each of the workers it immediately calls the appropriate `postMessage()` call to pass in both the buffer as well as the identifier for the thread. This results in five different threads that we care about; namely the main thread and threads that we've nicknamed 0, 1, 2, and 3.

JavaScript creates those threads, and the underlying engine goes to work assembling resources, allocating memory, and otherwise doing a lot of magic for us behind the scenes. The amount of time that it takes to perform those tasks is nondeterministic, which is unfortunate. We can't know that, for example, it always takes 100 ms to complete the preparation work. In fact, this number will change wildly across machines depending on things like core count and how busy the machine happens to be at the time the code is run. Lucky for us, the postMessage() call is essentially queued up for us; the JavaScript engine will call the worker's onmessage function once it's ready.

After that, the main thread finishes its work, then waits half a second (500 ms) using setTimeout, and finally calls Atomics.notify(). What would happen if the setTimeout value were too low, say 10 ms? Or even if it were called in the same stack outside of setTimeout? In that case the threads wouldn't yet be initialized, the worker wouldn't have had time to call Atomics.wait(), and the call would immediately return with a 0. What would happen if the time value is too high? Well, the application might be painfully slow, or any timeout value used by Atomics.wait() might have been exceeded.

On Thomas's laptop the threshold of readiness seems to be somewhere around 120 ms. At that point some of the threads are ready and some aren't. At about 100 ms usually none of the threads are ready, and at 180 ms usually all of the threads are ready. But *usually* is a word that we don't like to use in programming. It is difficult to know an exact amount of time before a thread is ready. Often this is an issue when first starting an application, not one that is present throughout the life cycle of the application.

To finish off the application, create a file named *worker.js*, and add the content from Example 5-3 to it.

Example 5-3. ch5-notify-order/worker.js

```
self.onmessage = ({data: {buffer, name}}) => {
  const view = new Int32Array(buffer);
  console.log(`Worker ${name} started`);
  const result = Atomics.wait(view, 0, 0, 1000); ❶
  console.log(`Worker ${name} awoken with ${result}`);
};
```

❶ Wait on 0th entry in buffer, assuming initial value of 0, for up to 1 second.

The worker accepts the shared buffer and the name of the worker thread and stores the values, printing a message that the thread has been initialized. It then calls Atomics.wait() using the 0th index of the buffer. It assumes an initial value of 0 is present in the buffer (which it is, since we haven't modified the value). The method call also uses a timeout value of one second (1,000 ms). Finally, once the method call is complete, the value is printed in the terminal.

Once you've finished creating these files, switch to a terminal and run another web server to view the content. Again, you can do so by running the following command:

```
$ npx MultithreadedJSBook/serve .
```

As usual, navigate to the URL printed in the terminal and open the console. If you don't see any output, you may need to refresh the page to run the application again. Table 5-2 contains the output from a test run.

Table 5-2. Example nondeterministic output

Log	Location
Worker 1 started	worker.js:4:11
Worker 0 started	worker.js:4:11
Worker 3 started	worker.js:4:11
Worker 2 started	worker.js:4:11
Worker 0 awoken with ok	worker.js:7:11
Worker 3 awoken with ok	worker.js:7:11
Worker 1 awoken with ok	worker.js:7:11
Worker 2 awoken with timed-out	worker.js:7:11

You will most likely get different output. In fact, if you refresh the page again, you may get different output once again. Or you may even get consistent output across multiple runs. Ideally, though, the final worker name that is printed with the "started" messages will also be the worker that fails with the "timed-out" message.

This output might be a little confusing. Earlier we stated that the order seems to be FIFO ordered, but the numbers here aren't from 0 to 3. The reason is that the order doesn't depend on the order that the threads were created (0, 1, 2, 3), but the order in which the threads executed the `Atomics.wait()` call (1, 0, 3, 2 in this case). Even with that in mind the order of the "awoken" messages is confusing (0, 3, 1, 2 in this case). This is likely due to a race condition in the JavaScript engine where different threads print messages, likely at almost the exact same moment.

Once printed, the messages don't get displayed directly to the screen. If that could happen, then the messages could overwrite each other, and you'd end up with visual tearing of pixels. Instead, the engine queues up the messages to be printed, and some other mechanism internal to the browser, but hidden away from us developers, determines the order in which they're taken from the queue and printed to the screen. For that reason, the order of the two sets of messages won't necessarily correlate. But the only way to truly tell any order is that the message that times out happens to be from the final thread that was started. Indeed, in this case the "timed-out" message is always from the last worker that was started.

Detecting Thread Preparedness

This experiment begs the question: how can an application deterministically know when a thread has finished going through initial setup and is thus prepared to take on work?

A simple way to do so is to call `postMessage()` from within the worker threads to post back to the parent thread at some point during the `onmessage()` handler. This works because once the `onmessage()` handler has been called the worker thread has finished its initial setup and is now running JavaScript code.

Here's an example of the quickest way to pull this off. First, copy the *ch5-notify-order/* directory you created and paste it as a new *ch5-notify-when-ready/* directory. Inside this directory the *index.html* file will remain the same, though the two JavaScript files will be updated. First, update *main.js* to contain the content from Example 5-4.

Example 5-4. ch5-notify-when-ready/main.js

```
if (!crossOriginIsolated) throw new Error('Cannot use SharedArrayBuffer');

const buffer = new SharedArrayBuffer(4);
const view = new Int32Array(buffer);
const now = Date.now();
let count = 4;

for (let i = 0; i < 4; i++) { ❶
  const worker = new Worker('worker.js');
  worker.postMessage({buffer, name: i}); ❷
  worker.onmessage = () => {
    console.log(`Ready; id=${i}, count=${--count}, time=${Date.now() - now}ms`);
    if (count === 0) { ❸
      Atomics.notify(view, 0);
    }
  };
}
```

❶ Instantiate four workers.

❷ Immediately post a message to the workers.

❸ Notify on the 0th entry once all four workers reply.

The script has been modified so that `Atomics.notify()` will be called after each of the four workers has posted a message back to the main thread. Once the fourth and final worker has posted a message, the notification is then sent. This allows the application to post a message as soon as it's ready, likely saving hundreds of milliseconds in the best case, and preventing a failure in the worst case (like when running the code on a very slow single-core computer).

The `Atomics.notify()` call has also been updated to simply wake up all threads instead of just three, and the timeout has been set back to the default of `Infinity`. This was done to show that every thread will receive the message on time.

Next, update *worker.js* to contain the content from Example 5-5.

Example 5-5. ch5-notify-when-ready/worker.js

```
self.onmessage = ({data: {buffer, name}}) => {
  postMessage('ready'); ❶
  const view = new Int32Array(buffer);
  console.log(`Worker ${name} started`);
  const result = Atomics.wait(view, 0, 0); ❷
  console.log(`Worker ${name} awoken with ${result}`);
};
```

❶   Post message back to parent thread to signal readiness.

❷   Wait for notification on the 0th entry.

This time the `onmessage` handler immediately calls `postMessage()` to send a message back to the parent. Then, the wait call happens shortly afterward. Technically, if the parent thread were to somehow receive the message before the `Atomics.wait()` call were made, then the application could conceivably break. But the code is relying on the fact that message passing is far slower than iterating over lines of code within a synchronous JavaScript function.

One thing to keep in mind is that calling `Atomics.wait()` will pause the thread. This means `postMessage()` can't be called afterward.

When you run this code, the new logs print out three pieces of information: the name of the thread, the countdown (always in the order of 3, 2, 1, 0), and finally the amount of time it took for the thread to be ready since the start of the script. Run the same command that you ran before and open the resulting URL in your browser. Table 5-3 contains the log output from some sample runs.

Table 5-3. Thread start timing

Firefox v88	Chrome v90
T1, 86ms	T0, 21ms
T0, 99ms	T1, 24ms
T2, 101ms	T2, 26ms
T3, 108ms	T3, 29ms

In this case, with a 16-core laptop, Firefox seems to take around four times as long to initialize the worker threads as Chrome does. Also, Firefox gives a more random thread order than Chrome. Each time the page is refreshed the order of threads for Firefox changes but the order in Chrome does not. This then suggests that the V8 engine used by Chrome is more optimized for starting new JavaScript environments or instantiating browser APIs than the SpiderMonkey engine used by Firefox.

Be sure to test this code in multiple browsers to compare the results that you get. Another thing to keep in mind is that the speed that it takes to initialize threads will also likely depend on the number of cores available on your computer. In fact, to have some additional fun with this program, change the value of 4 that is assigned to the count variable and in the for loop to a higher number, then run the code and see what happens. Upon increasing the value to 128, the amount of time it took both browsers to initialize threads jumped a lot. This also consistently breaks the order in which the threads are prepared on Chrome. Generally, performance is lost when using too many threads, and this is examined in more detail in "Low Core Count" on page 172.

Example Application: Conway's Game of Life

Now that we've had a look at Atomics.wait() and Atomics.notify(), it's time to look at a concrete example. We'll use Conway's Game of Life, a well-established concept that naturally lends itself to parallel programming. The "game" is actually a simulation of population growth and decay. The "world" this simulation exists in is a grid of cells that are in one of two states: alive or dead. The simulation works iteratively, and on each iteration, the following algorithm is performed for each cell.

1. If the cell is alive:

    a. If there are 2 or 3 neighbors alive, the cell remains alive.

    b. If there are 0 or 1 neighbors alive, the cell dies (this simulates underpopulation as a cause of death).

    c. If there are 4 or more neighbors alive, the cell dies (this simulates overpopulation as a cause of death).

2. If the cell is dead:

   a. If there are exactly 3 neighbors alive, the cell becomes alive (this simulates reproduction).

   b. In any other case, the cell remains dead.

When talking about "neighbors alive," we're referring to any cell that's at most one unit away from the current cell, including diagonals, and we're referring to the state prior to the current iteration. We can simplify these rules to the following.

1. If there are exactly 3 neighbors alive, the new cell state is alive (regardless of how it started).

2. If the cell is alive and exactly 2 neighbors are alive, the cell remains alive.

3. In all other cases, the new cell state is dead.

For our implementation, we'll make the following assumptions:

- The grid is a square. This is a slight simplification so that there's one less dimension to worry about.

- The grid wraps around itself like a torus. This means that when we're at an edge, and we need to evaluate a neighboring cell outside the bounds, we'll look at the cell at the other end.

We'll write our code for web browsers, since they give us a handy canvas element with which to plot the state of the Game of Life world. That being said, it's relatively straightforward to adapt the example to other environments that have some kind of image rendering. In Node.js you could even write to the terminal using ANSI escape codes.

Single-Threaded Game of Life

To start off, we'll build up a Grid class, which holds our Game of Life world as an array and handles each iteration. We'll build it in a frontend-agnostic way, and we'll even make it usable without any changes in our multithreaded example. To properly simulate the Game of Life, we'll need a multidimensional array to represent our grid of cells. We could use arrays of arrays, but to make things easier later on, we'll store it in a one-dimensional array (in fact, a Uint8Array), and then for any cell with coordinates x and y, we'll store it in the array at cells[size * x + y]. We'll also need two of these, since one will be for the current state, and one for the previous state. In another attempt to simplify things for later on, we'll store both of them sequentially in the same ArrayBuffer.

Make a directory called *ch5-game-of-life/* and add the contents of Example 5-6 to *gol.js* in that directory.

Example 5-6. ch5-game-of-life/gol.js (part 1)

```
class Grid {
  constructor(size, buffer, paint = () => {}) {
    const sizeSquared = size * size;
    this.buffer = buffer;
    this.size = size;
    this.cells = new Uint8Array(this.buffer, 0, sizeSquared);
    this.nextCells = new Uint8Array(this.buffer, sizeSquared, sizeSquared);
    this.paint = paint;
  }
```

Here we've started off the Grid class with a constructor. It takes in a size, which is the width of our square, an ArrayBuffer called buffer, and a paint function which we'll use later on. We then establish our cells and nextCells as instances of Uint8Array stored side-by-side in the buffer.

Next, we can add the cell retrieval method we'll need later on when performing iterations. Add the code in Example 5-7.

Example 5-7. ch5-game-of-life/gol.js (part 2)

```
  getCell(x, y) {
    const size = this.size;
    const sizeM1 = size - 1;
    x = x < 0 ? sizeM1 : x > sizeM1 ? 0 : x;
    y = y < 0 ? sizeM1 : y > sizeM1 ? 0 : y;
    return this.cells[size * x + y];
  }
```

To retrieve a cell with a given set of coordinates, we need to normalize the indices. Recall that we're saying the grid wraps around. The normalization we've done here makes sure that if we're one unit above or below the range, we instead retrieve the cell at the other end of the range.

Now, we'll add the actual algorithm that runs on every iteration. Add the code in Example 5-8.

Example 5-8. ch5-game-of-life/gol.js (part 3)

```
  static NEIGHBORS = [ ❶
    [-1, -1], [-1, 0], [-1, 1], [0, -1], [0, 1], [1, -1], [1, 0], [1, 1]
  ];

  iterate(minX, minY, maxX, maxY) { ❷
```

```
    const size = this.size;

    for (let x = minX; x < maxX; x++) {
      for (let y = minY; y < maxY; y++) {
        const cell = this.cells[size * x + y];
        let alive = 0;
        for (const [i, j] of Grid.NEIGHBORS) {
          alive += this.getCell(x + i, y + j);
        }
        const newCell = alive === 3 || (cell && alive === 2) ? 1 : 0;
        this.nextCells[size * x + y] = newCell;
        this.paint(newCell, x, y);
      }
    }

    const cells = this.nextCells;
    this.nextCells = this.cells;
    this.cells = cells;
  }
}
```

❶ The set of neighbors coordinates are used in the algorithm to look at neighboring
    cells in eight directions. We'll keep this array handy because we'll need to use it
    for every cell.

❷ The `iterate()` method takes in a range to operate on in the form of minimum X
    and Y values (inclusive) and maximum X and Y values (exclusive). For our
    single-threaded example, it will always be (0, 0, size, size), but putting a
    range here will make it easier to split up when we move to a multithreaded
    implementation, where we'll use these X and Y boundaries to divide the whole
    grid into sections for each thread to work on.

We loop over every cell in the grid, and for each one get the number of neighbors that
are alive. We're using the number 1 to represent living cells and 0 to represent dead
cells, so we can count the number of neighboring living cells by adding them all up.
Once we have that, we can apply the simplified Game of Life algorithm. We store the
new cell state in the `nextCells` array, and then provide the new cell state and coordinates to the `paint` callback for visualization. Then we swap the `cells` and `nextCells`
arrays for the subsequent iteration to use. That way, inside each iteration, `cells`
always represents the previous iteration's result, and `newCells` always represents the
current iteration's result.

All the code up until this point will be shared with our multithreaded implementation. With the `Grid` class complete, we can now move on to creating and initializing a
`Grid` instance and tying it to our UI. Add the code from Example 5-9.

Example 5-9. ch5-game-of-life/gol.js (part 4)

```
const BLACK = 0xFF000000; ❶
const WHITE = 0xFFFFFFFF;
const SIZE = 1000;

const iterationCounter = document.getElementById('iteration'); ❷
const gridCanvas = document.getElementById('gridcanvas');
gridCanvas.height = SIZE;
gridCanvas.width = SIZE;
const ctx = gridCanvas.getContext('2d');
const data = ctx.createImageData(SIZE, SIZE); ❸
const buf = new Uint32Array(data.data.buffer);

function paint(cell, x, y) { ❹
  buf[SIZE * x + y] = cell ? BLACK : WHITE;
}

const grid = new Grid(SIZE, new ArrayBuffer(2 * SIZE * SIZE), paint); ❺
for (let x = 0; x < SIZE; x++) { ❻
  for (let y = 0; y < SIZE; y++) {
    const cell = Math.random() < 0.5 ? 0 : 1;
    grid.cells[SIZE * x + y] = cell;
    paint(cell, x, y);
  }
}

ctx.putImageData(data, 0, 0); ❼
```

❶ We assign some constants for the black-and-white pixels we'll draw to the screen and set the size (actually, the width) of the grid we're using. Feel free to play around with the size to see the Game of Life play out in different magnitudes.

❷ We grab an iteration counter and canvas element from the HTML (which we'll write later on). We'll set our canvas width and height to SIZE, and get a 2D context from it to work with.

❸ We'll use an ImageData instance to modify the pixels on the canvas directly, via a Uint32Array.

❹ This paint() function will be used both in initialization of the grid and on each iteration to modify the buffer backing the ImageData instance. If a cell is alive, it'll paint it black. Otherwise, it'll paint it white.

❺ Now we create the grid instance, passing in the size, an ArrayBuffer big enough to hold both cells and nextCells, and our paint() function.

❻ To initialize the grid, we'll loop over all the cells and assign each one a random dead or alive state. At the same time, we'll pass the result to our paint() function to ensure that the image is updated.

❼ Whenever an ImageData is modified, we need to add it back to the canvas, so we're doing it here now that we're done initializing.

Finally, we're ready to start running iterations. Add the code from Example 5-10.

Example 5-10. ch5-game-of-life/gol.js (part 5)

```
let iteration = 0;
function iterate(...args) {
  grid.iterate(...args);
  ctx.putImageData(data, 0, 0);
  iterationCounter.innerHTML = ++iteration;
  window.requestAnimationFrame(() => iterate(...args));
}

iterate(0, 0, SIZE, SIZE);
```

For each iteration, we start off by calling our grid.iterate() method, which modifies the cells as appropriate. Note that it calls the paint() function for each cell, so once that happens, our image data is already set, so we just need to add it to the canvas context with putImageData(). Then, we'll update the iteration counter on the page and schedule another iteration to happen in a requestAnimationFrame() callback. Finally, we kick everything off with an initial call to iterate().

We're done with the JavaScript, but now we need the supporting HTML. Fortunately, this is very short. Add the contents of Example 5-11 to a file called *gol.html* in the same directory, and then open that file up in your browser.

Example 5-11. ch5-game-of-life/gol.html

```
<h3>Iteration: <span id="iteration">0</span></h3>
<canvas id="gridcanvas"></canvas>
<script src="gol.js"></script>
```

You should now see a 1,000 by 1,000 image displaying Conway's Game of Life, going through the iterations as fast as it can. It should look something like Figure 5-1.

Depending on your computer, you may find that this lags a little bit, rather than being crisp and smooth. Iterating over all of these cells and performing calculations on them takes a lot of computing power. To speed things up a bit, let's take advantage of some more CPU cores on your machine using web worker threads.

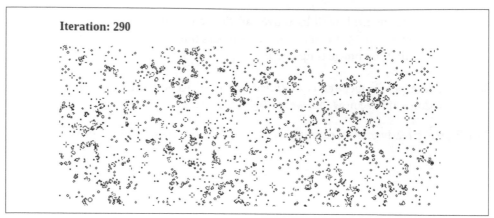

Figure 5-1. Conway's Game of Life after 290 iterations

Multithreaded Game of Life

For the multithreaded version of our Game of Life implementation, we can reuse a lot of the code. In particular, the HTML doesn't change and neither does our Grid class. We'll set up some worker threads and an additional one to coordinate and modify image data. We need that additional thread because we can't use Atomics.wait() on the main browser thread. We'll make use of SharedArrayBuffer, rather than the regular ArrayBuffer used in the single-threaded example. To coordinate the threads, we'll need 8 bytes for coordination, specifically 4 to synchronize in each direction, since Atomics.wait() requires at least an Int32Array. Since our coordination thread will also be generating the image data, we'll also need enough shared memory to hold that as well. For a grid of side length SIZE, this means a SharedArrayBuffer with memory laid out as in Table 5-4.

Table 5-4. Memory layout for four worker threads

Purpose	# of Bytes
Cells (or next cells)	SIZE * SIZE
Cells (or next cells)	SIZE * SIZE
Image data	4 * SIZE * SIZE
Worker thread wait	4
Coordination thread wait	4

To get started here, copy the *.html* and *.js* files from the previous example to new files named *thread-gol.html* and *thread-gol.js*, respectively. Edit *thread-gol.html* to make reference to this new JavaScript file.

Delete everything after the `Grid` class definition. The next thing we'll do is set up some constants. Add Example 5-12 to *thread-gol.js*.

Example 5-12. ch5-game-of-life/thread-gol.js (part 1)

```
const BLACK = 0xFF000000;
const WHITE = 0xFFFFFFFF;
const SIZE = 1000;
const THREADS = 5; // must be a divisor of SIZE

const imageOffset = 2 * SIZE * SIZE
const syncOffset = imageOffset + 4 * SIZE * SIZE;

const isMainThread = !!self.window;
```

The `BLACK`, `WHITE`, and `SIZE` constants have the same purpose as in the single-threaded example. We'll set this `THREADS` constant to any number that's a divisor of `SIZE`, and it will represent the number of worker threads we'll spawn for doing the Game of Life calculation. We'll be dividing the grid into chunks that can be handled by each thread. Feel free to play around with the `THREADS` and `SIZE` variables, so long as `THREADS` divides `SIZE`. We'll need the offsets for where the image data and sync bytes are stored, so those are handled here as well. Finally, we're going to use the same file to run on the main thread and any worker threads, so we'll need a way of knowing whether we're on the main thread or not.

Next, we'll start writing the code for the main thread. Add the contents of Example 5-13.

Example 5-13. ch5-game-of-life/thread-gol.js (part 2)

```
if (isMainThread) {
  const gridCanvas = document.getElementById('gridcanvas');
  gridCanvas.height = SIZE;
  gridCanvas.width = SIZE;
  const ctx = gridCanvas.getContext('2d');
  const iterationCounter = document.getElementById('iteration');

  const sharedMemory = new SharedArrayBuffer(    ❶
    syncOffset + // data + imageData
    THREADS * 4 // synchronization
  );
  const imageData = new ImageData(SIZE, SIZE);
  const cells = new Uint8Array(sharedMemory, 0, imageOffset);
  const sharedImageBuf = new Uint32Array(sharedMemory, imageOffset);
  const sharedImageBuf8 =
    new Uint8ClampedArray(sharedMemory, imageOffset, 4 * SIZE * SIZE);

  for (let x = 0; x < SIZE; x++) {
```

```
  for (let y = 0; y < SIZE; y++) {
    // 50% chance of cell being alive
    const cell = Math.random() < 0.5 ? 0 : 1;
    cells[SIZE * x + y] = cell;
    sharedImageBuf[SIZE * x + y] = cell ? BLACK : WHITE;
  }
}

imageData.data.set(sharedImageBuf8);
ctx.putImageData(imageData, 0, 0);
```

❶ The `SharedArrayBuffer` ends 16 bytes later than the `syncOffset`, since we need 4 bytes for synchronization for each of our four threads.

The first part of this is roughly the same as in the single-threaded example. We're just grabbing the DOM elements and setting the grid size. Next, we set up the `SharedArrayBuffer`, which we're calling `sharedMemory`, and put views on it for the `cells` (which we'll assign values to soon) and got the image data. We'll use both a `Uint32Array` and a `Uint8ClampedArray` for the image data, for modification and assignment to the `ImageData` instance, respectively.

Then we'll initialize the grid randomly, and at the same time modify the image data accordingly and populate that image data to the canvas context. This sets up our initial state for the grid. At this point, we can start spawning worker threads. Add the contents of Example 5-14.

Example 5-14. ch5-game-of-life/thread-gol.js (part 3)

```
const chunkSize = SIZE / THREADS;
for (let i = 0; i < THREADS; i++) {
  const worker = new Worker('thread-gol.js', { name: `gol-worker-${i}` });
  worker.postMessage({
    range: [0, chunkSize * i, SIZE, chunkSize * (i + 1)],
    sharedMemory,
    i
  });
}

const coordWorker = new Worker('thread-gol.js', { name: 'gol-coordination' });
coordWorker.postMessage({ coord: true, sharedMemory });

let iteration = 0;
coordWorker.addEventListener('message', () => {
  imageData.data.set(sharedImageBuf8);
  ctx.putImageData(imageData, 0, 0);
  iterationCounter.innerHTML = ++iteration;
  window.requestAnimationFrame(() => coordWorker.postMessage({}));
});
```

We set up some worker threads in a loop. For each one, we give it a unique name for debugging purposes, post it a message telling it what range (i.e., the boundaries minX, minY, maxX, and maxY) of the grid we want it to operate in, and send it the sharedMemory. Then we add a coordination worker, pass it the sharedMemory, and let it know that it's the coordination worker via a message.

From the main browser thread, we're only going to talk to this coordination worker. We'll set it up so that it loops by posting a message every time it receives one, but only after grabbing the image data from SharedMemory, making the appropriate UI updates, and requesting an animation frame.

The rest of the code runs in the other threads. Add the contents of Example 5-15.

Example 5-15. ch5-game-of-life/thread-gol.js (part 4)

```
} else {
  let sharedMemory;
  let sync;
  let sharedImageBuf;
  let cells;
  let nextCells;

  self.addEventListener('message', initListener);

  function initListener(msg) {
    const opts = msg.data;
    sharedMemory = opts.sharedMemory;
    sync = new Int32Array(sharedMemory, syncOffset);
    self.removeEventListener('message', initListener);
    if (opts.coord) {
      self.addEventListener('message', runCoord);
      cells = new Uint8Array(sharedMemory);
      nextCells = new Uint8Array(sharedMemory, SIZE * SIZE);
      sharedImageBuf = new Uint32Array(sharedMemory, imageOffset);
      runCoord();
    } else {
      runWorker(opts);
    }
  }
```

We're on the other side of that isMainThread condition now, so we know we're in a worker thread or the coordination thread. Here, we declare some variables, and then add an initial listener to the message event. Regardless of whether this is a coordination thread or a worker thread, we'll need the sharedMemory and sync variables populated, so we assign those in the listener. Then we remove the initialization listener, since we won't need it anymore. The worker threads won't rely on message passing at all, and the coordination thread will have a different listener, as we'll see in a moment.

If we've initialized a coordination thread we'll add a new message listener; a runCoord function that we'll define later. Then we'll get references to cells and nextCells since we'll need to keep track on the coordination thread separate from what's going on in the Grid instances in the worker threads. Since we're generating the image on the coordination thread, we'll need that too. Then we run the first iteration of runCoord. If we've initialized a worker thread, we simply go ahead and pass the options (containing the range to operate) to runWorker().

Let's go ahead and define runWorker() right now. Add the contents of Example 5-16.

Example 5-16. ch5-game-of-life/thread-gol.js (part 5)

```
function runWorker({ range, i }) {
  const grid = new Grid(SIZE, sharedMemory);
  while (true) {
    Atomics.wait(sync, i, 0);
    grid.iterate(...range);
    Atomics.store(sync, i, 0);
    Atomics.notify(sync, i);
  }
}
```

Worker threads are the only ones that need an instance of the Grid class, so first we instantiate it, passing in the sharedMemory as the backing buffer. This works because we decided that the first part of the sharedMemory would be the cells and next Cells, as it would be in the single-threaded example.

Then we start an infinite loop. The loop performs the following operations:

1. It performs an Atomics.wait() on the ith element of the sync array. In the coordination thread, we'll do the appropriate Atomics.notify() to allow this to proceed. We're waiting for the coordination thread here because otherwise we may start changing data and swapping references to cells and nextCells before other threads are ready and data has made its way to the main browser thread.

   Then it performs the iteration on the Grid instance. Remember, we're only operating on the range that the coordination thread said to operate on via the range property.

2. Once that's done, it notifies the main thread of having completed this task. This is done by setting the ith element of the sync array to 1 with Atomics.store(), and then waking the waiting thread via Atomics.notify(). We're using the transition away from the 0 state as an indicator that we should do some work, and a transition back to the 0 state to notify that we've finished the work.

We're using `Atomics.wait()` to stop the coordination thread from executing while the worker threads are modifying data, and then stop the worker threads with `Atomics.wait()` while the coordination thread does its work. On either side, we use `Atomics.notify()` to wake the other thread and immediately go back into a waiting state, waiting for the other thread to notify back. Because we use atomic operations to both modify data and control when it is modified, we know that all the data accesses are *sequentially consistent*. In the interleaving program flow across threads, a deadlock cannot occur, since we're always flipping execution back and forth from the coordination thread to the worker threads. The worker threads never execute on the same parts of memory as each other, so we don't have to worry about this concept from the perspective of solely the worker threads.

Worker threads can just run infinitely. We don't have to be worried about that infinite loop because it will only proceed if `Atomics.wait()` returns, which requires that another thread calls `Atomics.notify()` for that same array element.

Let's wrap up the code here with the `runCoord()` function, which is triggered via a message from the main browser thread after the initialization message. Add the contents of Example 5-17.

Example 5-17. ch5-game-of-life/thread-gol.js (part 6)

```
function runCoord() {
  for (let i = 0; i < THREADS; i++) {
    Atomics.store(sync, i, 1);
    Atomics.notify(sync, i);
  }
  for (let i = 0; i < THREADS; i++) {
    Atomics.wait(sync, i, 1);
  }
  const oldCells = cells;
  cells = nextCells;
  nextCells = oldCells;
  for (let x = 0; x < SIZE; x++) {
    for (let y = 0; y < SIZE; y++) {
      sharedImageBuf[SIZE * x + y] = cells[SIZE * x + y] ? BLACK : WHITE;
    }
  }
  self.postMessage({});
}
```

The first thing that happens here is the coordination thread notifying the worker threads via the `i`th element of the `sync` array for each worker thread, waking them up to perform an iteration. When they're done, they'll notify via the same element of the `sync` array, so we'll wait on those. The fact that each of these calls to `Atomics.wait()`

blocks the thread execution is exactly why we need this coordination thread in the first place, rather than just doing it all on the main browser thread.

Next, we swap the `cells` and `nextCells` references. The workers have already done this for themselves inside the `iterate()` method, so we need to follow suit here. Then we're ready to iterate over all the `cells` and convert their values to pixels in the image data. Finally, we post a message back to the main browser thread, indicating that the data is ready to be displayed in the UI. The coordination thread has nothing to do until the next time it receives a message, at which point `runCoord` is run again. This method completes the conceptual loop started in Example 5-14.

Now we're done! To view the HTML file, remember that in order to use `SharedArray Buffer`, we need a server running with particular headers set. To do this, run the following in your *ch5-game-of-life* directory:

```
$ npx MultithreadedJSBook/serve .
```

Then, append */thread-gol.html* to the URL provided to see our multithreaded implementation of Conway's Game of Life running. Because we haven't changed any UI code, it should look exactly the same as the single-threaded example in Figure 5-1. The only difference you should see is in performance. The transitions between iterations likely appear to be much smoother and quicker. You're not imagining things! We've moved the work of calculating cell states and plotting pixels into separate threads, so now the main thread is free to animate more smoothly, and iterations happen faster because we're using more CPU cores in parallel to do the work.

Most importantly, we're avoiding most of the overhead of passing messages between threads for coordination by just using `Atomics.notify()` to let other threads know that they can continue after having paused themselves with `Atomics.wait()`.

Atomics and Events

At the heart of JavaScript lies the event loop, which allows the language to create new call stacks and handle events. It's always been there and we JavaScript engineers have always depended on it. This is true for both JavaScript that runs in the browser, where you might have jQuery that listens for a click event in the DOM, or JavaScript that runs on the server, where you might have the Fastify server that waits for an incoming TCP connection to be established.

Enter the new kid on the block: `Atomics.wait()` and shared memory. This pattern now allows applications to halt the execution of JavaScript, thereby causing the event loop to completely stop working. Because of this you can't simply start throwing calls to make use of multithreading into your application and expect it to work without problem. Instead, certain restrictions must be followed to make the application behave nicely.

One such restriction is hinted at when it comes to browsers: the main thread of the application should not call `Atomics.wait()`. And, while it can be done in a simple Node.js script, you should really avoid doing so in a larger application. For example, if your main Node.js thread is handling incoming HTTP requests, or has a handler for receiving operating system signals, what's going to happen when the event loop comes to a halt when a wait operation is started? Example 5-18 is an example of such a program.

Example 5-18. ch5-node-block/main.js

```
#!/usr/bin/env node

const http = require('http');

const view = new Int32Array(new SharedArrayBuffer(4));
setInterval(() => Atomics.wait(view, 0, 0, 1900), 2000); ❶

const server = http.createServer((req, res) => {
  res.end('Hello World');
});

server.listen(1337, (err, addr) => {
  if (err) throw err;
  console.log('http://localhost:1337/');
});
```

❶ Every 2 seconds the app pauses for 1.9 seconds

If you feel so inclined, create a directory for this file and execute the server by running the following command:

```
$ node main.js
```

Once it's running, execute the following command in your terminal several times, waiting a random amount of time between each invocation:

```
$ time curl http://localhost:1337
```

What this application does is first create an HTTP server and listen for requests. Then, every two seconds, a call to `Atomics.wait()` is made. It's configured in such a way that the application freezes for 1.9 seconds to exaggerate the effect of long pauses. The `curl` command you're running is prefixed with the `time` command, which displays the amount of time the following command takes to run. Your output will then randomly vary between 0 and 1.9 seconds, which is a huge amount of time for a web request to pause for. Even as you reduce that timeout value closer and closer to 0, you'll still end up with micro stutters that globally affect all incoming requests. If web browsers allowed `Atomics.wait()` calls in the main thread, you would definitely be encountering micro stutters from this in websites you visit today.

Another question still remains: what sort of restrictions should come into play with each of the additional threads that an application spawns, considering that each thread has their own event loop?

Our recommendation is to designate ahead of time what the main purpose of each spawned thread is. Each thread either becomes a CPU-heavy thread that makes heavy use of `Atomics` calls or an event-heavy thread that makes minimal `Atomics` calls. With such an approach, you might have a thread that is a worker in the truest sense, constantly performing complex calculations and writing the results to a shared array buffer. You would also have your main thread, which is then mostly communicating via message passing and doing event loop based work. It then might make sense to have simple intermediary threads that call `Atomics.wait()` as they wait for another thread to finish doing work, then call `postMessage()` to send the resulting data back to the main thread to handle the result at a much higher level.

To summarize the concepts in this section:

- Don't use `Atomics.wait()` in the main thread.
- Designate which threads are CPU-heavy and use lots of `Atomics` calls and which threads are evented.
- Consider using simple "bridge" threads to wait and post messages where appropriate.

These are some very high-level guidelines that you can follow when designing your application. But sometimes some more concrete patterns really help drive the point home. Chapter 6 contains some such patterns you might find beneficial.

Multithreaded Patterns

The JavaScript APIs that expose multithreading are, on their own, really quite basic with the functionality they provide. As you saw in Chapter 4, the purpose of the SharedArrayBuffer is to store a raw, binary representation of data. Even Chapter 5 continued this pattern with the Atomics object, exposing rather primitive methods for coordinating or modifying a handful of bytes at a time.

Just looking at such abstract and low-level APIs can make it difficult to see the big picture, or what these APIs can really be used for. It's admittedly difficult to take these concepts and convert them into something that is genuinely useful for an application. That's what this chapter is for.

This chapter contains popular design patterns for implementing multithreaded functionality inside an application. These design patterns take inspiration from the past, as each of them existed long before JavaScript was even invented. Though working demos of them are likely available in many forms, such as C++ textbooks, translating them for use with JavaScript isn't always straightforward.

By examining these patterns you'll get a much better feel for how the applications you develop can benefit from multithreading.

Thread Pool

The thread pool is a very popular pattern that is used in most multithreaded applications in some form or another. Essentially, a *thread pool* is a collection of homogeneous worker threads that are each capable of carrying out CPU-intensive tasks that the application may depend on. This differs somewhat from the approach you've been using so far where usually a single worker thread, or a finite number of workers, has been used. As an example of this, the libuv library that Node.js depends on provides a thread pool, defaulting to four threads, for performing low-level I/O operations.

This pattern might feel similar to distributed systems that you may have worked with in the past. For example, with a container orchestration platform, there's usually a collection of machines that are each capable of running application containers. With such a system each machine might have different capabilities, such as running different operating systems or having different memory and CPU resources. When this happens, the orchestrator may assign points to each machine based on resources and applications, then consume said points. On the other hand, a thread pool is much simpler because each worker is capable of carrying out the same work and each thread is just as capable as the other since they're all running on the same machine.

The first question when creating a thread pool is how many threads should be in the pool?

Pool Size

There are essentially two types of programs: those that run in the background, like a system daemon process, which ideally shouldn't consume that many resources, and programs that run in the foreground that any given user is more likely to be aware of, like a desktop application or a web server. Browser applications are usually constrained to running as foreground applications, whereas Node.js applications are free to run in the background—though Node.js is most commonly used to build servers, frequently as the only process inside a container. In either case, the intent with a JavaScript application is often to be the main focus at a particular point in time, and any computations necessary to achieve the purpose of the program should ideally be executed as soon as possible.

To execute instructions as quickly as possible, it makes sense to break them up and run them in parallel. To maximize CPU usage it figures that each of the cores in a given CPU should be used, as equally as possible, by the application. Thus, the number of CPU cores available to the machine should be a determining factor for the number of threads—aka workers—an application should use.

Typically, the size of a thread pool won't need to dynamically change throughout the lifetime of an application. Usually there's a reason the number of workers is chosen, and that reason doesn't often change. That's why you'll work with a thread pool with a fixed size, dynamically chosen when the application launches.

Here is the idiomatic approach for getting the number of threads available to the currently running JavaScript application, depending on whether the code runs inside a browser or inside a Node.js process:

```
// browser
cores = navigator.hardwareConcurrency;
```

```
// Node.js
cores = require('os').cpus().length;
```

One thing to keep in mind is that with most operating systems there is not a direct correlation between a thread and a CPU core. For example, when running an application with four threads on a CPU with four cores, it's not like the first core is always handling the first thread, the second core the second thread, and so forth. Instead, the operating system constantly moves tasks around, occasionally interrupting a running program to handle the work of another application. In a modern operating system there are often hundreds of background processes that need to be occasionally checked. This often means that a single CPU core will be handling the work of more than one thread.

Each time a CPU core switches focus between programs—or threads of a program—a small context shift overhead comes into play. Because of this, having too many threads compared to the number of CPU cores can cause a loss of performance. The constant context switching will actually make an application slower, so applications should attempt to reduce the number of threads clamoring for attention from the OS. However, having too few threads can then mean that an application takes too long to do its thing, resulting in a poor user experience or otherwise wasted hardware.

Another thing to keep in mind is that if an application makes a thread pool with four workers, then the minimum number of threads that application is using is five because the main thread of the application also comes into play. There are also background threads to consider, like the libuv thread pool, a garbage collection thread if the JavaScript engine employs one, the thread used to render the browser chrome, and so on. All of these will affect the performance of the application.

The characteristics of the application itself will also affect the ideal size of a thread pool. Are you writing a cryptocurrency miner that does 99.9% of the work in each thread and almost no I/O and no work in the main thread? In that case using the number of available cores as the size of the thread pool might be OK. Or are you writing a video streaming and transcoding service that performs heavy CPU and heavy I/O? In that case, you may want to use the number of available cores minus two. You'll need to perform benchmarks with your application to find the perfect number, but a reasonable starting point might be to use the number of available cores minus one and then tweak when necessary.

Once you have determined the number of threads to use, you're ready to determine how to dispatch work to the workers.

Dispatch Strategies

Because the goal of a thread pool is to maximize the work that can be done in parallel, it stands to reason that no single worker should get too much work to handle and no threads should be sitting there idle without work to do. A naive approach might be to just collect tasks to be done, then pass them in once the number of tasks ready to be performed meets the number of worker threads and continue once they all complete. However, each task isn't guaranteed to take the same amount of time to complete. It could be that some are very fast, taking milliseconds, and others may be slow, taking seconds or longer. A more robust solution must therefore be built.

A few strategies are often employed by applications to dispatch tasks to workers in a worker pool. These strategies draw parallels to those used by reverse proxies for the purpose of sending requests to backend services. Here's a list of the most common strategies:

Round robin

> Each task is given to the next worker in the pool, wrapping around to the beginning once the end has been hit. So, with a pool size of three, the first task goes to Worker 1, then Worker 2, then Worker 3, then back to Worker 1, and so on. The benefit of this is that each thread gets the exact same number of tasks to perform, but the drawback is that if the complexities of each task is a multiple of the number of threads (like each 6th task takes a long time to perform), then there will be an unfair distribution of work. The HAProxy reverse proxy refers to this as `round robin`.

Random

> Each task is assigned to a random worker in the pool. Although this is the simplest to build, being entirely stateless, it can also mean that some of the workers are sometimes given too much work to perform, and others will sometimes be given too little work to perform.

Least busy

> A count of the number of tasks being performed by each worker is maintained, and when a new task comes along it is given to the least busy worker. This can even be extrapolated so that each worker only has a single task to perform at a time. When two workers have a tie for the least amount of work, then one can be chosen randomly. This is perhaps the most robust approach, especially if each task consumes the same amount of CPU, but it does require the most effort to implement. If some tasks use fewer resources, such as if a task calls `setTimeout()`, then it can lead to skew in worker workloads. HAProxy refers to this as `leastconn`.

Other strategies employed by reverse proxies might have a nonobvious implementation that could be made in your applications as well. For example, HAProxy has a strategy for load balancing called source, which takes a hash of the client's IP address and uses that to consistently route requests to a single backend. An equivalent to this might be useful in cases where worker threads maintain an in-memory cache of data and routing-related tasks to the same worker could result in more cache hits, but such an approach is a little harder to generalize.

 Depending on the nature of your application, you may find that one of these strategies offers much better performance than the others. Again, benchmarking is your friend when it comes to measuring a given application's performance.

Example Implementation

This example repurposes the existing files from *ch2-patterns/* that you created in "Putting It All Together" on page 47, but a lot of the error handling has been removed for brevity, and the code has been made compatible with Node.js. Create a new directory named *ch6-thread-pool/* to house the files that you'll create in this section.

The first file you'll create is *main.js*. This is the entrypoint into the application. The previous version of this code just used a Promise.allSettled() call to add tasks to the pool, but that's not all that interesting because it adds everything at the same time. Instead, this application exposes a web server, and every request then creates a new task for the thread pool. With this approach, previous tasks might have been completed by the time the pool is consulted, which then results in more interesting patterns like with a real-world application.

Add the content from Example 6-1 to *main.js* to start off your application.

Example 6-1. ch6-thread-pool/main.js

```
#!/usr/bin/env node
const http = require('http');
const RpcWorkerPool = require('./rpc-worker.js');
const worker = new RpcWorkerPool('./worker.js',
  Number(process.env.THREADS), ❶
  process.env.STRATEGY); ❷

const server = http.createServer(async (req, res) => {
  const value = Math.floor(Math.random() * 100_000_000);
  const sum = await worker.exec('square_sum', value);
  res.end(JSON.stringify({ sum, value }));
});

server.listen(1337, (err) => {
```

```
    if (err) throw err;
    console.log('http://localhost:1337/');
});
```

❶ The THREADS environment variable controls the pool size.

❷ The STRATEGY environment variable sets the dispatch strategy.

This application used two environment variables to make it easy to experiment with. The first is named THREADS and will be used to set the number of threads in the thread pool. The second environment variable is STRATEGY, which can be used to set the thread pool dispatch strategy. Otherwise, the server isn't too exciting, as it just uses the built-in http module. The server listens on port 1337, and any request, regardless of path, triggers the handler. Each request calls the square_sum command defined in the workers while passing in a value between 0 and 100 million.

Next, create a file named *worker.js*, and add the content from Example 6-2 to it.

Example 6-2. ch6-thread-pool/worker.js

```
const { parentPort } = require('worker_threads');

function asyncOnMessageWrap(fn) {
  return async function(msg) {
    parentPort.postMessage(await fn(msg));
  }
}

const commands = {
  async square_sum(max) {
    await new Promise((res) => setTimeout(res, 100));
    let sum = 0; for (let i = 0; i < max; i++) sum += Math.sqrt(i);
    return sum;
  }
};

parentPort.on('message', asyncOnMessageWrap(async ({ method, params, id }) => ({
  result: await commands[method](...params), id
}))));
```

This file isn't too interesting because it's essentially a simplified version of the *worker.js* file that you previously created. A lot of the error handling was removed to make the code shorter (feel free to add it back if you like), and the code has also been modified to be compatible with the Node.js APIs. In this example only a single command remains, namely square_sum.

Next, create a file named *rpc-worker.js*. This file is going to be quite large and has been broken up into smaller sections. First, add the content from Example 6-3 to it.

Example 6-3. ch6-thread-pool/rpc-worker.js (part 1)

```
const { Worker } = require('worker_threads');
const CORES = require('os').cpus().length;
const STRATEGIES = new Set([ 'roundrobin', 'random', 'leastbusy' ]);

module.exports = class RpcWorkerPool {
  constructor(path, size = 0, strategy = 'roundrobin') {
    if (size === 0)      this.size = CORES; ❶
    else if (size < 0)   this.size = Math.max(CORES + size, 1);
    else                 this.size = size;

    if (!STRATEGIES.has(strategy)) throw new TypeError('invalid strategy');
    this.strategy = strategy; ❷
    this.rr_index = -1;

    this.next_command_id = 0;
    this.workers = []; ❸
    for (let i = 0; i < this.size; i++) {
      const worker = new Worker(path);
      this.workers.push({ worker, in_flight_commands: new Map() }); ❹
      worker.on('message', (msg) => {
        this.onMessageHandler(msg, i);
      });
    }
  }
}
```

❶ The thread pool size is highly configurable.

❷ The strategy is validated and stored.

❸ An array of workers is maintained instead of just one.

❹ The in_flight_commands list is now maintained per worker.

This file starts off by requiring the worker_threads core module to create workers, as well as the os module to get the number of available CPU cores. After that the RpcWor kerPool class is defined and exported. Next, the constructor for the class is provided. The constructor takes three arguments, with the first being the path to the worker file, the second being the size of the pool, and the third being the strategy to use.

The pool size is highly configurable and allows the caller to provide a number. If the number is positive, then it is used as the size of the pool. The default value is zero, and if provided, the number of CPU cores is used for the pool size. If a negative number is provided, then that number is subtracted from the number of available cores and that is used instead. So, on an 8 core machine, passing in a pool size of −2 would result in a pool size of 6.

The strategy argument may be one of roundrobin (the default), random, or leastbusy. The value is validated before being assigned to the class. The rr_index value is used as the round robin index and is a number that cycles through the next available worker ID.

The next_command_id is still global across all threads, so the first command will be 1 and the next will be 2, regardless of whether the commands are both handled by the same worker thread or not.

Finally, the workers class property is an array of workers instead of the previous singular worker property. The code to handle it is largely the same, but the in_flight_commands list is now local to the individual workers, and the ID of the worker is passed as an additional argument to the onMessageHandler() method. This is because the individual worker will later need to be looked up when a message is sent back to the main process.

Continue editing the file by adding the content from Example 6-4 to it.

Example 6-4. ch6-thread-pool/rpc-worker.js (part 2)

```
onMessageHandler(msg, worker_id) {
  const worker = this.workers[worker_id];
  const { result, error, id } = msg;
  const { resolve, reject } = worker.in_flight_commands.get(id);
  worker.in_flight_commands.delete(id);
  if (error) reject(error);
  else resolve(result);
}
```

This part of the file defines the onMessageHandler() method that is called when a worker sends a message back to the main thread. It's mostly the same as before, except this time it accepts an additional argument, worker_id, which is used to look up the worker that sent the message. Once it looks up the worker, it handles the promise rejection/resolve and removes the entry from the list of pending commands.

Continue editing the file by adding the content from Example 6-5 to it.

Example 6-5. ch6-thread-pool/rpc-worker.js (part 3)

```
exec(method, ...args) {
  const id = ++this.next_command_id;
  let resolve, reject;
  const promise = new Promise((res, rej) => { resolve = res; reject = rej; });
  const worker = this.getWorker(); ❶
```

```
    worker.in_flight_commands.set(id, { resolve, reject });
    worker.worker.postMessage({ method, params: args, id });
    return promise;
  }
```

❶ The applicable worker is looked up.

This chunk of the file defines the exec() method, which is what the application calls when it wants to execute a command in one of the workers. Again, it's largely unchanged, but this time it calls the getWorker() method to get the appropriate worker to handle the next command, instead of working with a single default worker. That method is defined in the next section.

Finish editing the file by adding the content from Example 6-6 to it.

Example 6-6. ch6-thread-pool/rpc-worker.js (part 4)

```
getWorker() {
  let id;
  if (this.strategy === 'random') {
    id = Math.floor(Math.random() * this.size);
  } else if (this.strategy === 'roundrobin') {
    this.rr_index++;
    if (this.rr_index >= this.size) this.rr_index = 0;
    id = this.rr_index;
  } else if (this.strategy === 'leastbusy') {
    let min = Infinity;
    for (let i = 0; i < this.size; i++) {
      let worker = this.workers[i];
      if (worker.in_flight_commands.size < min) {
        min = worker.in_flight_commands.size;
        id = i;
      }
    }
  }
  console.log('Selected Worker:', id);
  return this.workers[id];
}
};
```

This final chunk of the file defines a final, new method named getWorker(). This method considers the strategy that was defined for the class instance when determining which worker to use next. The bulk of the function is a large if statement where each branch correlates to a strategy.

The first one, random, doesn't require any additional state, making it the simplest. All the function does is to randomly choose one of the entries in the pool and then choose that as a candidate.

The second branch, for roundrobin, is slightly more complicated. This one makes use of a class property named rr_index, incrementing the value and then returning the worker located at the new index. Once the index exceeds the number of workers, it then wraps back around to zero.

The final branch, for leastbusy, has the most complexity. It works by looping through each one of the workers, noting the number of commands that it currently has in progress by looking at the size of the in_flight_commands map, and determining if it's the smallest value that has been encountered so far. If so, it then decides that worker is the next to be used. Note that this implementation will stop at the first matching worker with the lowest number of in-flight commands; so the first time it runs it will always choose worker 0. A more robust implementation might look at all of the candidates with the lowest, equal commands, and choose one randomly. The chosen worker ID is logged so that you can tell what's happening.

Now that your application has been prepared, you're ready to execute it. Open up two terminal windows and navigate to the *ch6-thread-pool/* directory in the first one. In this terminal window execute the following command:

```
$ THREADS=3 STRATEGY=leastbusy node main.js
```

This starts a process with a thread pool containing three workers using the leastbusy strategy.

Next, run the following command in the second terminal window:

```
$ npx autocannon -c 5 -a 20 http://localhost:1337
```

This executes the autocannon command, which is an npm package for performing benchmarks. In this case, though, you're not actually running a benchmark, but you're instead just running a whole bunch of queries. The command is configured to open five connections at a time and send a total of 20 requests. Essentially, this will make 5 requests seemingly in parallel, then as the requests are closed the remaining 15 requests will be made. This is akin to a production web server you might build.

Since the application is using the leastbusy strategy, and because the code is written to choose the first process with the fewest commands, the first five requests should then essentially be treated as round robin. With a pool size of three, when the application first runs, each worker has zero tasks. So the code first elects to use Worker 0. For the second request, the first worker has one task while the second and third worker have zero, so the second is chosen. Then the third. For the fourth, each of the three workers is consulted, each having one task, and so the first is chosen again.

After the first five tasks are assigned, the remaining worker assignments are essentially random, as each command takes essentially a random amount of time to succeed.

Next, kill the server using Ctrl+C, and then run it again using the roundrobin strategy:

```
$ THREADS=3 STRATEGY=roundrobin node main.js
```

Run the same autocannon command as before in the second terminal. This time you should see that the tasks are always executed in the order of 0, 1, 2, 0, and so on.

Finally, kill the server with Ctrl+C again, and run it again with the random strategy:

```
$ THREADS=3 STRATEGY=random node main.js
```

Run the autocannon command a final time and note the results. This time it should be entirely random. If you notice the same worker getting chosen multiple times in a row, it likely means that worker is overloaded.

Table 6-1 contains sample output from a previous run of this experiment. Each column corresponds to a new request, and the number in the table contains the ID of the worker that was chosen to serve the request.

Table 6-1. Example thread pool strategy output

Strategy	R1	R2	R3	R4	R5	R6	R7	R8	R9	R10
Least busy	0	1	2	0	1	0	1	2	1	0
Round robin	0	1	2	0	1	2	0	1	2	0
Random	2	0	1	1	0	0	0	1	1	0

In this particular run the random approach hardly ever used the worker with an ID of 2.

Mutex: A Basic Lock

A mutually exclusive lock, or *mutex*, is a mechanism for controlling access to some shared data. It ensures that only one task may use that resource at any given time. Here, a task can mean any sort of concurrent task, but most often the concept is used when working with multiple threads, to avoid race conditions. A task *acquires* the lock in order to run code that accesses the shared data, and then *releases* the lock once it's done. The code between the acquisition and the release is called the *critical section*. If a task attempts to acquire the lock while another task has it, that task will be blocked until the other task releases the lock.

It may not be obvious why you might want to use a mutex when we have atomic operations at our disposal through the Atomics object. Surely it's more efficient to use atomic operations to modify and read data, since we're blocking other operations for shorter time periods, right? It turns out that code often requires that data not be modified externally across more than one operation. Put another way, the units of atomicity provided by atomic operations are too small for many algorithms' critical sections. For example, two integers may be read from several parts of shared memory, then summed up to be written to another part. If values are changed in between the two retrievals, the sum will reflect values from two different tasks, which can lead to logic errors later on in the program.

Let's look at an example program that initializes a buffer with a bunch of numbers and performs some basic math on them in several threads. We'll have each thread grab a value at a unique index per thread, then grab a value from a shared index, multiply those together, and write them at the shared index. Then we'll read from that shared index and check that it's equal to the product of the previous two reads. In between the two reads, we'll perform a busy loop to simulate doing some other work that takes some time.

Make a directory called *ch6-mutex* and put the contents of Example 6-7 into a file called *thread_product.js*.

Example 6-7. ch6-mutex/thread-product.js

```
const {
  Worker, isMainThread, workerData
} = require('worker_threads');
const assert = require('assert');

if (isMainThread) {
  const shared = new SharedArrayBuffer(4 * 4); ❶
  const sharedInts = new Int32Array(shared);
  sharedInts.set([2, 3, 5, 7]);
  for (let i = 0; i < 3; i++) {
    new Worker(__filename, { workerData: { i, shared } });
  }
} else {
  const { i, shared } = workerData;
  const sharedInts = new Int32Array(shared);
  const a = Atomics.load(sharedInts, i);
  for (let j = 0; j < 1_000_000; j++) {}
  const b = Atomics.load(sharedInts, 3);
  Atomics.store(sharedInts, 3, a * b);
  assert.strictEqual(Atomics.load(sharedInts, 3), a * b); ❷
}
```

❶ We'll be using three threads and an `Int32Array` to hold the data, so we need it big enough to hold three 32-bit integers, plus a fourth to be the shared multiplier/result.

❷ Here, we're checking our work. In a real-world application, there likely would be no check here, but this simulates depending on the result to perform other actions, which may happen later on in the program.

You can run this example as follows:

```
$ node thread-product.js
```

You might find that on the first try, or even the first bunch of tries, this works fine, but go ahead and keep running it. Alternatively you may find that the assertion fails immediately. At some point, within the first 20 or so attempts, you should see that the assertion fails. While we're using atomic operations, we're using four of them, and between any of these, some change can occur in these values. This is a classic example of a race condition. All the threads are reading and writing concurrently (though not in parallel, since the operations themselves are atomic), so the results aren't deterministic for given input values.

To solve this, we'll implement a `Mutex` class using the primitives we have in `Atomics`. We'll be making use of `Atomics.wait()` to wait until the lock can be acquired, and `Atomics.notify()` to notify threads that the lock has been released. We'll use `Atomics.compareExchange()` to swap the locked/unlocked state and determine whether we need to wait to get the lock. Create a file in the same directory called *mutex.js* and add the contents of Example 6-8 to get started on the `Mutex` class.

Example 6-8. ch6-mutex/mutex.js (part 1)

```
const UNLOCKED = 0;
const LOCKED = 1;

const {
  compareExchange, wait, notify
} = Atomics;

class Mutex {
  constructor(shared, index) {
    this.shared = shared;
    this.index = index;
  }
```

Here we've defined our `LOCKED` and `UNLOCKED` states as 1 and 0, respectively. Really, they can be any values that fit in the `TypedArray` we pass into the `Mutex` constructor, but sticking with 1 and 0 makes it easier to think about as a boolean value. We have set up the constructor to take in two values that will be assigned to properties: the TypedArray we'll be operating on, and the index in that array that we'll use as the lock status. Now, we're ready to start using Atomics to add the acquire() method, which uses the destructured Atomics. Add the acquire() method from Example 6-9.

Example 6-9. ch6-mutex/mutex.js (part 2)

```
acquire() {
  if (compareExchange(this.shared, this.index, UNLOCKED, LOCKED) === UNLOCKED) {
    return;
  }
  wait(this.shared, this.index, LOCKED);
  this.acquire();
}
```

To acquire a lock, we make an attempt to swap the UNLOCKED state for the LOCKED state at the mutex's array index, using Atomics.compareExchange(). If the swap is successful, then there's nothing left to do and we've acquired the lock, so we can just return. Otherwise we need to wait for unlocking, which in this case means waiting for notification that the value change from LOCKED to anything else. Then we make another attempt to acquire the lock. We're doing this through recursion here to illustrate the "retry" nature of the operation, but it could just as easily be a loop. It should work on the second time through since we've specifically waited for it to become unlocked, but in between the wait() and the compareExchange(), the value may have changed, so we need to check again. In a real-world implementation, you might want to both add a timeout on the wait() and limit the number of attempts that can be made.

 In many production mutex implementations, in addition to the "unlocked" and "locked" states, you'll often find a state meaning "locked and contended." *Contention* arises when one thread attempts to acquire a lock that's already held by another thread. By keeping track of this state, the mutex code can avoid using extra notify() calls, allowing for better performance.

Semaphores

The element in the shared array that we use to represent the state of being locked or unlocked is a trivial example of a *semaphore*. Semaphores are variables used to convey state information between threads. They indicate a count of a resource being used. In the case of a mutex, we limit this to 1, but semaphores in other scenarios may involve other limits for other purposes.

Now we'll look at releasing a lock. Add the release() method shown in Example 6-10.

Example 6-10. ch6-mutex/mutex.js (part 3)

```
release() {
  if (compareExchange(this.shared, this.index, LOCKED, UNLOCKED) !== LOCKED) {
    throw new Error('was not acquired');
  }
  notify(this.shared, this.index, 1);
}
```

Here we're using Atomics.compareExchange() to swap the locked state again, much as we did to acquire the lock. This time, we want to make sure that the original state was indeed LOCKED since we don't want to release the lock if we haven't acquired it. The only thing left to do at this point is to notify(), enabling a waiting thread (if there is one) to acquire the lock. We set the count for notify() to 1, because there's no need to wake more than one sleeping thread, since only one can ever hold the lock at one time.

What we have now is enough to work as a serviceable mutex lock. However, it's relatively easy to acquire a lock and forget to release it, or in some other way have an unexpected critical section. For many use cases, the critical section is well-defined and knowable ahead of time. In those cases, it makes sense to have a helper method on the Mutex class to wrap critical sections with ease. Let's do exactly that by adding the exec() method in Example 6-11, which will also finish off the class.

Example 6-11. ch6-mutex/mutex.js (part 4)

```
  exec(fn) {
    this.acquire();
    try {
      return fn();
    } finally {
      this.release();
    }
  }
}

module.exports = Mutex;
```

All we're doing here is calling the passed-in function and returning its value, but wrapping that with an acquire() beforehand and release() afterward. This way the passed-in function contains all the code of our critical section. Note that we call the passed-in function inside a try block, with the release() happening in the corresponding finally. Since the passed-in function could throw an exception, we want to make sure that we release the lock even in that scenario. This completes our `Mutex` class, so now we can move on to using it in our example.

Make a copy of *thread-product.js* in the same directory, called *thread-product-mutex.js*. In that file `require` the *mutex.js* file and assign it to a `const` called `Mutex`. Add another 4 bytes to the `SharedArrayBuffer` (e.g., `new SharedArrayBuffer(4 * 5)`) for our lock to use, then replace everything in the `else` block with the contents of Example 6-12.

Example 6-12. ch6-mutex/thread-product-mutex.js

```
const { i, shared } = workerData;
const sharedInts = new Int32Array(shared);
const mutex = new Mutex(sharedInts, 4); ❶
mutex.exec(() => {
  const a = sharedInts[i]; ❷
  for (let j = 0; j < 1_000_000; j++) {}
  const b = sharedInts[3];
  sharedInts[3] = a * b;
  assert.strictEqual(sharedInts[3], a * b);
});
```

❶ Before this line, everything's the same as when we weren't using the mutex. Now, we'll initialize one, using the fifth element of our `Int32Array` as our lock data.

❷ Inside the function passed to `exec()`, we're in our critical section, which is protected by the lock. This means we don't need atomic operations to read or manipulate the array. Instead, we can just operate on it like any other `TypedArray`.

In addition to enabling ordinary array access techniques, the mutex has allowed us to ensure that no other thread is able to modify these pieces of data while we're looking at them. Because of that, our assertion would never fail. Give it a try! Run the following command to run this example, and even run it tens, hundreds, or even thousands of times. It will never fail the assertion like the version using only atomics did:

```
$ node thread-product-mutex.js
```

 Mutexes are straightforward tools to lock access to a resource. They allow critical sections to operate without interference from other threads. They are one example of how we can leverage combinations of atomic operations to make new building blocks for multithreaded programming. In the next section, "Streaming Data with Ring Buffers" on page 137, we'll put this building block to some practical use.

Streaming Data with Ring Buffers

Many applications involve streaming data. For example, HTTP requests and responses are usually presented via HTTP APIs as sequences of byte data coming in as chunks as they are received. In network applications, data chunks are size-constrained by packet sizes. In filesystem applications, data chunks can be size-constrained by kernel buffer sizes. Even if we output data to these resources without any regard for streaming, the kernel will break the data up into chunks in order to send it to its destination in a buffered manner.

Streaming data also occurs in user applications and can be used as a way to transfer larger amounts of data between computation units, like processes or threads. Even without separate computation units, you may want or need to hold data in some kind of buffer before processing it. This is where *ring buffers*, also known as *circular buffers*, come in handy.

A ring buffer is an implementation of a first-in-first-out (FIFO) queue, implemented using a pair of indices into an array of data in memory. Crucially, for efficiency, when data is inserted into the queue, it won't ever move to another spot in memory. Instead, we move the indices around as data gets added to or removed from the queue. The array is treated as if one end is connected to the other, creating a ring of data. This means that if these indices are incremented past the end of the array, they'll go back to the beginning.

An analog in the physical world is the restaurant order wheel, commonly found in North American diners. In restaurants using this kind of system, the wheel is usually placed in a part of the restaurant that divides the customer-facing area from the kitchen. Orders are taken from the customers on note papers, which are then inserted into the wheel in order. Then, on the kitchen side, the cooks can grab orders off the wheel in the same order so that food is cooked in the appropriate order, and no customer is left waiting too long for their food. This is a bounded[1] FIFO queue, just like our ring buffers. Indeed, it's also literally circular!

To implement a ring buffer, we'll need the two indices, head and tail. The head index refers to the next position to add data into the queue, and the tail index refers to the next position to read data out of the queue from. When data is written to or read

---

1 In practice, restaurants can get much busier than what the order wheel can handle. Restaurants will often solve this with such tricks as inserting more than one order paper in the same slot on the wheel, with some agreed-upon ordering in each slot. In the case of our ring buffers, we can't shove more than one piece of data into an array slot, so we can't use the same hack. Instead, a more complete system should have a way of indicating that the queue is full and can't handle any more data right now. As you'll see, we're going to do exactly that.

from the queue, we increase the `head` or `tail` index, respectively, by the amount of data written or read, modulo the size of the buffer.

Figure 6-1 visualizes how a ring buffer works using a ring with a 16-byte buffer. The first diagram contains 4 bytes of data, starting at Byte 0 (where the tail is located) and ending at Byte 3 (with head one byte ahead at Byte 4). Once four bytes of data are added to the buffer, the head marker moves forward four bytes to Byte 8, shown in the second diagram. In the final diagram, the first four bytes have been read, so the tail moves to Byte 4.

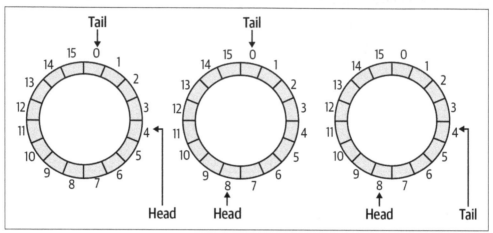

Figure 6-1. Writing data moves the head forward, while reading data moves the tail forward

Let's make an implementation of a ring buffer. We'll start off not worrying about threads, but to make our lives easier later on, we'll store `head` and `tail` as well as the current `length` of the queue in a `TypedArray`. We could try just using the difference between `head` and `tail` as the length, but that leaves us with an ambiguous case, where we can't tell if the queue is empty or full when the `head` and `tail` are the same value, so we'll have a separate value for `length`. We'll start by setting up the constructor and acessors, by adding the contents of Example 6-13 to a file called *ch6-ring-buffer/ring-buffer.js*.

Example 6-13. ch6-ring-buffer/ring-buffer.js (part 1)

```
class RingBuffer {
  constructor(meta/*: Uint32Array[3]*/, buffer /*: Uint8Array */) {
    this.meta = meta;
    this.buffer = buffer;
  }

  get head() {
```

```
    return this.meta[0];
  }

  set head(n) {
    this.meta[0] = n;
  }

  get tail() {
    return this.meta[1];
  }

  set tail(n) {
    this.meta[1] = n;
  }

  get length() {
    return this.meta[2];
  }

  set length(n) {
    this.meta[2] = n;
  }
```

The constructor takes in a three-element Uint32Array called meta, which we'll use for our head, tail, and length. For convenience, we've also added those properties as getters and setters, which internally just access those array elements. It also takes in a Uint8Array that will be the backing storage for our ring buffer. Next, we'll add the write() method. Add the method as defined in Example 6-14.

Example 6-14. ch6-ring-buffer/ring-buffer.js (part 2)

```
  write(data /*: Uint8Array */) { ❶
    let bytesWritten = data.length;
    if (bytesWritten > this.buffer.length - this.length) { ❷
      bytesWritten = this.buffer.length - this.length;
      data = data.subarray(0, bytesWritten);
    }
    if (bytesWritten === 0) {
      return bytesWritten;
    }
    if (
      (this.head >= this.tail && this.buffer.length - this.head >= bytesWritten) ||
      (this.head < this.tail && bytesWritten <= this.tail - this.head) ❸
    ) {
      // Enough space after the head. Just write it in and increase the head.
      this.buffer.set(data, this.head);
      this.head += bytesWritten;
    } else { ❹
      // We need to split the chunk into two.
      const endSpaceAvailable = this.buffer.length - this.head;
```

```
    const endChunk = data.subarray(0, endSpaceAvailable);
    const beginChunk = data.subarray(endSpaceAvailable);
    this.buffer.set(endChunk, this.head);
    this.buffer.set(beginChunk, 0);
    this.head = beginChunk.length;
  }
  this.length += bytesWritten;
  return bytesWritten;
}
```

❶ In order for this code to work correctly, `data` needs to be an instance of the same TypedArray as `this.buffer`. This can be checked via static type checking, or with an assertion, or both.

❷ If there's not enough space in the buffer for all the data to be written, we'll write as many bytes as we can to fill the buffer and return the number of bytes that were written. This notifies whoever is writing the data that they'll need to wait for some of the data to be read out of it before continuing to write.

❸ This conditional represents when we have enough *contiguous* space to write the data. This happens when either the head is after the tail in the array and the space after the head is bigger than the data to write, *or* when the head is before the tail and there's enough space between the tail and the head. For either of these conditions, we can just write the data to the array and increase the head index by the length of the data.

❹ On the other side of that `if` block, we need to write data until the end of the array and then wrap it around to write at the beginning of the array. This means splitting the data into a chunk to write at the end and a chunk to write at the beginning, and writing them accordingly. We're using `subarray()` rather than `slice()` to chop up the data to avoid unnecessary secondary copy operations.

Writing turns out to be just a matter of copying the bytes over using `set()` and changing the `head` index appropriately, with a special case for when the data is split across the boundaries of the array. Reading is very similar, as shown in the `read()` method in Example 6-15.

Example 6-15. ch6-ring-buffer/ring-buffer.js (part 3)

```
read(bytes) {
  if (bytes > this.length) { ❶
    bytes = this.length;
  }
  if (bytes === 0) {
    return new Uint8Array(0);
  }
```

```
    let readData;
    if (
      this.head > this.tail || this.buffer.length - this.tail >= bytes ❷
    ) {
      // The data is in a contiguous chunk.
      readData = this.buffer.slice(this.tail, bytes)
      this.tail += bytes;
    } else { ❸
      // Read from the end and the beginning.
      readData = new Uint8Array(bytes);
      const endBytesToRead = this.buffer.length - this.tail;
      readData.set(this.buffer.subarray(this.tail, this.buffer.length));
      readData.set(this.buffer.subarray(0, bytes - endBytesToRead), endBytesToRead);
      this.tail = bytes - endBytesToRead;
    }
    this.length -= bytes;
    return readData;
  }
}
```

❶ The input to read() is the number of bytes *requested*. If there aren't enough bytes in the queue, it will instead return all the bytes currently in the queue.

❷ If the requested data is in a contiguous chunk reading from the tail, we'll just give that directly to the caller using slice() to get a copy of those bytes. We'll move the tail to the end of the returned bytes.

❸ In the else case, the data is split across the boundaries of the array, so we need to get both chunks and stitch them together in reverse order. To do that, we'll allocate a big enough Uint8Array, then copy the data from the beginning and end of the array. The new tail is set to the end of the chunk at the beginning of the array.

When reading bytes out of the queue, it's important to *copy* them out, rather than just refer to the same memory. If we don't, then other data written to the queue might end up in these arrays at some time in the future, which is something we don't want. That's why we use slice() or a new Uint8Array for the returned data.

At this point, we have a working single-threaded bounded queue, implemented as a ring buffer. If we wanted to use it with one thread writing (the *producer*) and one thread reading (the *consumer*), we could use a SharedArrayBuffer as the backing storage for the inputs to constructor, pass that to another thread, and instantiate it there as well. Unfortunately, we haven't yet used any atomic operations or identified and isolated critical sections using locks, so if multiple threads use the buffer, we can end up with race conditions and bad data. We'll need to rectify this.

The read and write operations assume that none of the head, tail, or length are going to change by other threads throughout the operation. We may be able to get more specific than that later on, but being this general to start will at least give us the thread safety we need to avoid race conditions. We can use the `Mutex` class from "Mutex: A Basic Lock" on page 131 to identify critical sections and make sure they're only executed one at a time.

Let's require the `Mutex` class and add the wrapper class in Example 6-16 to the file that will make use of our existing `RingBuffer` class.

Example 6-16. ch6-ring-buffer/ring-buffer.js (part 4)

```
const Mutex = require('../ch6-mutex/mutex.js');

class SharedRingBuffer {
  constructor(shared/*: number | SharedArrayBuffer*/) {
    this.shared = typeof shared === 'number' ?
      new SharedArrayBuffer(shared + 16) : shared;
    this.ringBuffer = new RingBuffer(
      new Uint32Array(this.shared, 4, 3),
      new Uint8Array(this.shared, 16)
    );
    this.lock = new Mutex(new Int32Array(this.shared, 0, 1));
  }

  write(data) {
    return this.lock.exec(() => this.ringBuffer.write(data));
  }

  read(bytes) {
    return this.lock.exec(() => this.ringBuffer.read(bytes));
  }
}
```

To start it off, the constructor accepts or creates the `SharedArrayBuffer`. Notice that we add 16 bytes to the size of the buffer to handle both the `Mutex`, which needs a one-element `Int32Array`, and the `RingBuffer` metadata, which needs a three-element `Uint32Array`. We'll lay out the memory as in Table 6-2.

Table 6-2. SharedRingBuffer memory layout

Data	Type[Size]	SharedArrayBuffer Index
Mutex	Int32Array[1]	0
RingBuffer meta	Uint32Array[3]	4
RingBuffer buffer	Uint32Array[size]	16

The `read()` and `write()` operations are wrapped with the `exec()` method from the `Mutex`. Recall that this prevents any other critical sections protected by the same mutex from running at the same time. By wrapping them, we ensure that even if we have multiple threads both reading from and writing to the same queue, we won't have any race conditions from `head` or `tail` being modified externally in the middle of these critical sections.

To see this data structure in action, let's create some *producer* and *consumer* threads. We'll set up a `SharedRingBuffer` with 100 bytes to work with. The producer threads will write the string `"Hello, World!\n"` to the `SharedRingBuffer`, repeatedly, as fast as they can acquire the lock. The consumer threads will attempt to read 20 bytes at a time, and we'll log how many bytes they were able to read. The code to get this done is all in Example 6-17, which you can add to the end of *ch6-ring-buffer/ring-buffer.js*.

Example 6-17. ch6-ring-buffer/ring-buffer.js (part 5)

```
const { isMainThread, Worker, workerData } = require('worker_threads');
const fs = require('fs');

if (isMainThread) {
  const shared = new SharedArrayBuffer(116);
  const threads = [
    new Worker(__filename, { workerData: { shared, isProducer: true } }),
    new Worker(__filename, { workerData: { shared, isProducer: true } }),
    new Worker(__filename, { workerData: { shared, isProducer: false } }),
    new Worker(__filename, { workerData: { shared, isProducer: false } })
  ];
} else {
  const { shared, isProducer } = workerData;
  const ringBuffer = new SharedRingBuffer(shared);

  if (isProducer) {
    const buffer = Buffer.from('Hello, World!\n');
    while (true) {
      ringBuffer.write(buffer);
    }
  } else {
    while (true) {
      const readBytes = ringBuffer.read(20);
      fs.writeSync(1, `Read ${readBytes.length} bytes\n`); ❶
    }
  }
}
```

❶ You might notice that we're not using `console.log()` to write our byte counts to `stdout` and instead using a synchronous write to the file descriptor corresponding to `stdout`. This is because we're using an infinite loop without any `await` inside. We're starving the Node.js event loop, so with `console.log` or any other asynchronous logger, we'd never actually see any output.

You can run this example with Node.js as follows:

```
$ node ring-buffer.js
```

The output produced by this script will show the number of bytes read in each iteration in each consumer thread. Because we're asking for 20 bytes each time, you'll see that as the maximum number read. You'll see all zeros sometimes when the queue is empty. You'll see other numbers when the queue is partially full.

A number of things can be tweaked in our example. The size of the SharedRing Buffer, the number of producer and consumer threads, the size of the written message, and the number of bytes being attempted to be read all contribute to the throughput of data. As with anything else, it's always worth measuring and tweaking the values to find the optimal state for your application. Go ahead and try tweaking some of these in the example code and see how the output changes.

Lock-Free Queues

Our implementation of a ring buffer may be functionally sound, but it isn't the most efficient. In order to perform *any* operation on the data, all other threads are blocked from accessing the data. While this may be the simplest approach, solutions without using locks do exist, which instead take advantage of carefully used atomic operations for synchronization. The trade-off here is complexity.

Actor Model

The *actor model* is a programming pattern for performing concurrent computation that was first devised in the 1970s. With this model an *actor* is a primitive container that allows for executing code. An actor is capable of running logic, creating more actors, sending messages to other actors, and receiving messages.

These actors communicate with the outside world by way of message passing; otherwise, they have their own isolated access to memory. An actor is a first-class citizen in the Erlang programming language,[2] but it can certainly be emulated using JavaScript.

The actor model is designed to allow computations to run in a highly parallelized manner without necessarily having to worry about where the code is running or even the protocol used to implement the communication. Really, it should be transparent to program code whether one actor communicates with another actor locally or remotely. Figure 6-2 shows how actors can be spread out across processes and machines.

---

2 Another noteworthy implementation of the actor pattern is in the Scala language.

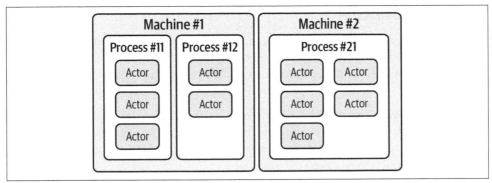

Figure 6-2. Actors can be spread across processes and machines

Pattern Nuances

Actors are able to process each message, or task, that they receive one at a time. When these messages are first received, they sit in a message queue, sometimes referred to as a mailbox. Having a queue is convenient because if two messages were received at once then they both shouldn't be processed at the same time. Without a queue, one actor might need to check if another actor is ready before sending a message, which would be a very tedious process.

Although no two actors are able to write to the same piece of shared memory, they are free to mutate their own memory. This includes maintaining state modifications over time. For example, an actor could keep track of the number of messages that it has processed, and then deliver that data in messages that it later outputs.

Because there's no shared memory involved, the actor model is able to avoid some of the multithreading pitfalls discussed earlier, such as race conditions and deadlocks. In many ways, an actor is like a function in a functional language, accepting inputs and avoiding access to global state.

Since actors handle a single task at a time they can often be implemented in a single-threaded fashion. And, while a single actor is only able to process a single task at a time, different actors are free to run code in parallel.

A system that uses actors shouldn't expect that messages are guaranteed to be ordered on a FIFO basis. Instead, it should be resilient to delays and out-of-order delivery, especially since actors can be spread across a network.

Individual actors can also have the concept of an address, which is a way to uniquely refer to a single actor. One way to represent this value could be to use a URI. For example, `tcp://127.0.0.1:1234/3` might refer to the third actor running in a program on the local computer listening on port 1234. The implementation covered here doesn't use such addresses.

Relating to JavaScript

The actors that exist as first-class citizens in languages such as Erlang can't be perfectly reproduced using JavaScript, but we can certainly try. There are likely dozens of ways to draw parallels and implement actors, and this section exposes you to one of them.

One draw of the actor model is that actors don't need to be limited to a single machine. This means that processes can run on more than one machine and communicate over the network. We can implement this using Node.js processes, each communicating using JSON via the TCP protocol.

Because individual actors should be able to run code in parallel with other actors, and each actor processes only a single task at a time, it then stands to reason that actors should probably run on different threads to maximize system usage. One way to go about this is to instantiate new worker threads. Another way would be to have dedicated processes for each actor, but that would use more resources.

Because there is no need to deal with shared memory between the different actors, the `SharedArrayBuffer` and `Atomics` objects can be largely ignored (though a more robust system might rely on them for coordination purposes).

Actors require a message queue so that while one message is being processed another message can wait until the actor is ready. JavaScript workers sort of handle this for us using the `postMessage()` method. Messages delivered in this manner wait until the current JavaScript stack is complete before grabbing the next message. If each actor is only running synchronous code, then this built-in queue can be used. On the other hand, if actors can perform asynchronous work, then a manual queue will need to be built instead.

So far the actor model might sound familiar to the thread pool pattern covered in "Thread Pool" on page 121. Indeed, there are a lot of similarities, and you can almost think of the actor model as a pool of thread pools. But there are enough differences that the two concepts are worth differentiating. Really, the actor model promises a unique paradigm for computing, truly a high-level programming pattern that can change the way you approach writing code. In practice, the actor model involves programs that often depend on thread pools.

Example Implementation

Create a new directory named *ch6-actors/* for this implementation. Inside this directory, copy and paste the existing *ch6-thread-pool/rpc-worker.js* file from Example 6-3 and the *ch6-thread-pool/worker.js* file from Example 6-2. Those files will be used as the basis of the thread pool in this example and can remain unchanged.

Next, create a file named *ch6-actors/server.js* and add the content from Example 6-18 to it.

Example 6-18. ch6-actors/server.js (part 1)

```
#!/usr/bin/env node

const http = require('http');
const net = require('net');

const [,, web_host, actor_host] = process.argv;
const [web_hostname, web_port] = web_host.split(':');
const [actor_hostname, actor_port] = actor_host.split(':');

let message_id = 0;
let actors = new Set(); // collection of actor handlers
let messages = new Map(); // message ID -> HTTP response
```

This file creates two server instances. The first is a TCP server, a rather basic protocol, while the second is an HTTP server, which is a higher-level protocol based on TCP, though the two server instances won't depend on each other. The first part of this file contains boilerplate for accepting command-line arguments to configure the two servers.

The `message_id` variable contains a number that will increment as each new HTTP request is made. The `messages` variable contains a mapping of message IDs to response handlers that will be used to reply to the messages. This is the same pattern that you used in "Thread Pool" on page 121. Finally, the `actors` variable contains a collection of handler functions that are used to send messages to external actor processes.

Next, add the content from Example 6-19 to the file.

Example 6-19. ch6-actors/server.js (part 2)

```
net.createServer((client) => {
  const handler = data => client.write(JSON.stringify(data) + '\0'); ❶
  actors.add(handler);
  console.log('actor pool connected', actors.size);
  client.on('end', () => {
    actors.delete(handler); ❷
    console.log('actor pool disconnected', actors.size);
  }).on('data', (raw_data) => {
    const chunks = String(raw_data).split('\0'); ❸
    chunks.pop(); ❹
    for (let chunk of chunks) {
      const data = JSON.parse(chunk);
      const res = messages.get(data.id);
```

```
      res.end(JSON.stringify(data) + '\0');
      messages.delete(data.id);
    }
  });
}).listen(actor_port, actor_hostname, () => {
  console.log(`actor: tcp://${actor_hostname}:${actor_port}`);
});
```

❶ A null byte '\0' is inserted between messages.

❷ When a client connection is closed, it is removed from the actors set.

❸ The data events may contain multiple messages and are split on null bytes.

❹ The final byte is a null byte, so the last entry in chunks is an empty string.

This file creates the TCP server. This is how dedicated actor processes will connect to the main server process. The net.createServer() callback is called each time an actor process connects. The client argument represents a TCP client, essentially a connection to the actor process. A message is logged each time a connection is made, and a handler function for conveniently messaging the actor is added to the actors collection.

When a client disconnects from the server, that client's handler function is deleted from the actors collection. Actors communicate with the server by sending messages over TCP, which triggers the data event.[3] The messages they send are JSON-encoded data. This data contains an id field which correlates to the message ID. When the callback is run, the correlating handler function is retrieved from the messages map. Finally, the response message is sent back to the HTTP request, the message is removed from the messages map, and the server listens on the specified interface and port.

The connection between the server and the actor pool client is a long-lived connection. That is why event handlers are set up for things like the data and end events.

---

3 Large messages, like if strings are being passed instead of a few small numbers, may get split across TCP messages and arrive in multiple data events. Keep this in mind if adapting this code for production use.

Notably missing from this file is an error handler for the client connection. Since it's missing, a connection error will cause the server process to terminate. A more robust solution would delete the client from the `actors` collection.

The `'\0'` null bytes are inserted between messages because when one side emits a message it's not guaranteed to arrive in a single `data` event on the other side. Notably, when multiple messages are sent in quick succession, they will arrive in a single `data` event. This is a bug you won't encounter while making single requests with `curl`, but that you would encounter when making many requests with `autocannon`. This results in multiple JSON documents concatenated together, like so: `{"id":1…}{"id":2…}`. Passing that value into `JSON.parse()` results in an error. The null bytes cause the events to resemble this: `{"id":1…}\0{"id":2…}\0`. The string is then split on the null byte and each segment is parsed separately. If a null byte were to appear in a JSON object, it would be escaped, meaning it's safe to use a null byte to separate JSON documents.

Next, add the content from Example 6-20 to the file.

Example 6-20. ch6-actors/server.js (part 3)

```
http.createServer(async (req, res) => {
  message_id++;
  if (actors.size === 0) return res.end('ERROR: EMPTY ACTOR POOL');
  const actor = randomActor();
  messages.set(message_id, res);
  actor({
    id: message_id,
    method: 'square_sum',
    args: [Number(req.url.substr(1))]
  });
}).listen(web_port, web_hostname, () => {
  console.log(`web:    http://${web_hostname}:${web_port}`);
});
```

This part of the file creates an HTTP server. Unlike the TCP server, each request represents a short-lived connection. The `http.createServer()` callback is called once for each HTTP request that is received.

Inside this callback the current message ID is incremented and the list of actors is consulted. If it's empty, which can happen when the server starts but an actor hasn't joined, an error message "ERROR: EMPTY ACTOR POOL" is returned. Otherwise, if actors are present, a random one is then chosen. This isn't the best approach, though — a more robust solution is discussed at the end of this section.

Next, a JSON message is sent to the actor. The message contains an `id` field which represents the message ID, a `method` field which represents the function to be called (always `square_sum` in this case), and finally the list of arguments. In this case the HTTP request path contains a slash and a number, like */42*, and the number is extracted to be used as the argument. Finally, the server listens on the provided interface and port.

Next, add the content from Example 6-21 to the file.

Example 6-21. ch6-actors/server.js (part 4)

```
function randomActor() {
  const pool = Array.from(actors);
  return pool[Math.floor(Math.random() * pool.length)];
}
```

This part of the file just grabs a random actor handler from the `actors` list.

With this file complete (for now), create a new file named *ch6-actors/actor.js*. This file represents a process that doesn't provide a server, but instead will connect to the other server process. Start the file off by adding the content from Example 6-22 to it.

Example 6-22. ch6-actors/actor.js (part 1)

```
#!/usr/bin/env node

const net = require('net');
const RpcWorkerPool = require('./rpc-worker.js');

const [,, host] = process.argv;
const [hostname, port] = host.split(':');
const worker = new RpcWorkerPool('./worker.js', 4, 'leastbusy');
```

Again, this file starts off with some boilerplate to extract the hostname and port information for the server process. It also initializes a thread pool using the `RpcWor` `kerPool` class. The pool has a strict size of four threads, which can be thought of as four actors, and uses the `leastbusy` algorithm.

Next, add the content from Example 6-23 to the file.

Example 6-23. ch6-actors/actor.js (part 2)

```
const upstream = net.connect(port, hostname, () => {
  console.log('connected to server');
}).on('data', async (raw_data) => {
  const chunks = String(raw_data).split('\0'); ❶
  chunks.pop();
  for (let chunk of chunks) {
    const data = JSON.parse(chunk);
    const value = await worker.exec(data.method, ...data.args);
```

```
    upstream.write(JSON.stringify({
      id: data.id,
      value,
      pid: process.pid
    }) + '\0');
  }
}).on('end', () => {
  console.log('disconnect from server');
});
```

❶ The actor also needs to handle null byte chunk separation.

The net.connect() method creates a connection to the upstream port and host-name, which represents the server process, logging a message once the connection succeeds. When the server sends a message to this actor, it triggers the data event, passing in a buffer instance as the raw_data argument. This data, containing a JSON payload, is then parsed.

The actor process then invokes one of its workers, calling the requested method and passing in the arguments. Once the worker/actor is finished, the data is then sent back to the server instance. The same message ID is preserved using the id property. This value must be provided because a given actor process can receive multiple message requests at the same time and the main server process needs to know which reply correlates with which request. The returned value is also provided in the message. The process ID is also provided as metadata in the response assigned to pid so that you can visualize which program is calculating what data.

Again, notably missing is proper error handling. If a connection error were to happen, you would see the process terminate entirely.

Figure 6-3 is a visualization of the implementation you've just built.

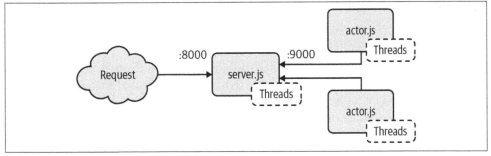

Figure 6-3. A visualization of the actor model implementation in this section

Now that your files are complete, you're ready to run your programs. First, run the server, providing a hostname and port to use for the HTTP server, followed by a hostname and port to use for the TCP server. You can do this by running the following command:

```
$ node server.js 127.0.0.1:8000 127.0.0.1:9000
# web:    http://127.0.0.1:8000
# actor: tcp://127.0.0.1:9000
```

In this case the process displays the two server addresses.

Next, send a request to the server in a new terminal window:

```
$ curl http://localhost:8000/9999
# ERROR: EMPTY ACTOR POOL
```

Whoops! In this case the server replied with an error. Since there are no running actor processes, there is nothing that can execute the work.

Next, run an actor process and give it the hostname and port for the server instance. You can do that by running the following command:

```
$ node actor.js 127.0.0.1:9000
```

You should see a message printed from both the server and the worker process that a connection was established. Next, run the `curl` command again in a separate terminal window:

```
$ curl http://localhost:8000/99999
# {"id":4,"value":21081376.519967034,"pid":160004}
```

You should get back a similar value to the one printed earlier. With the new actor process attached, the program went from having zero actors available to perform work to having four actors. But you don't need to stop there. In another terminal window run another instance of the worker using the same command, and issue another `curl` command:

```
$ node actor.js 127.0.0.1:9000
```

```
$ curl http://localhost:8000/8888888
# {"id":4,"value":21081376.519967034,"pid":160005}
```

As you run the command multiple times you should see that the `pid` value changes in the response. Congratulations, you've now dynamically increased the count of actors available to your application. This was done at runtime, effectively increasing the performance of your application without downtime.

Now, one of the benefits of the actor pattern is that it doesn't really matter where the code runs. In this case the actors live inside an external process. This allowed the error to happen when the server was first executed: an HTTP request was made, but an actor process hadn't yet connected. One way to fix this is to add some actors to the server process as well.

Modify the first *ch6-actors/server.js* file and add the content from Example 6-24 to it.

Example 6-24. ch6-actors/server.js (part 5, bonus)

```
const RpcWorkerPool = require('./rpc-worker.js');
const worker = new RpcWorkerPool('./worker.js', 4, 'leastbusy');
actors.add(async (data) => {
  const value = await worker.exec(data.method, ...data.args);
  messages.get(data.id).end(JSON.stringify({
    id: data.id,
    value,
    pid: 'server'
  }) + '\0');
  messages.delete(data.id);
});
```

This addition to the file creates a worker thread pool in the server process, effectively adding an additional four actors to the pool. Kill the existing server and actor processes that you've created with Ctrl+C. Then, run your new server code and send it a curl request:

```
$ node server.js 127.0.0.1:8000 127.0.0.1:9000
$ curl http://localhost:8000/8888888
# {"id":8,"value":17667693458.923462,"pid":"server"}
```

In this case the pid value has been hardcoded to server to signify that the process performing the calculation is the server process. Much like before, you can run some more actor processes to have them connect to the server and run more curl commands to send requests to the server. When this happens you should see that requests are handled either by dedicated actor processes or by the server.

With the actor pattern, you shouldn't think of the joined actors as external APIs. Instead, think of them as an extension of the program itself. This pattern can be powerful, and it comes with an interesting use case. *Hot code loading* is when newer versions of application code replaces old versions and is done while the application continues to run. With the actor pattern you've built, you are able to modify the *actor.js / worker.js* files, modify the existing square_sum() method, or even add new methods. Then, you can launch new actor programs and terminate old actor programs, and the main server will then start using the new actors.

Also worth noting is that the version of the actor model covered in this section does have several shortcomings that should be considered before implementing something like this in production. The first is that, although the individual actors within an actor process are chosen by which is least busy, the actor process itself is chosen randomly. This can lead to skewed workloads. To fix this you would need some sort of coordination mechanism to keep track of which actors are free.

Another shortcoming is that individual actors aren't addressable by other actors; in fact, one actor cannot call code from another actor. Architecturally, the processes resemble the star topology, where actor processes strictly connect to the server process. Ideally, all actors could connect with each other, and actors could individually address each other.

A big benefit of this approach is that of resilience. With the approach covered in this section there's only a single HTTP server. If the server process dies, then the whole application dies. A more resilient system might have each process be both an HTTP server and a TCP server, and have a reverse proxy route requests to all processes. Once these changes are made, you are closer to the actor model implementation provided by more robust platforms.

## CHAPTER 7

WebAssembly

While the title of this book is *Multithreaded JavaScript*, modern JavaScript runtimes also support WebAssembly. For the unaware, WebAssembly (often abbreviated as WASM) is a binary-encoded instruction format that runs on a stack-based virtual machine. It's designed with security in mind and runs in a sandbox where the only things it has access to are memory and functions provided by the host environment. The main motivation behind having such a thing in browsers and other JavaScript runtimes is to run the parts of your program that are performance-sensitive in an environment where execution can happen much faster than JavaScript. Another goal is to provide a compile target for typically compiled languages like C, C++, and Rust. This opens the door for developers of those languages to develop for the web.

Generally, the memory used by WebAssembly modules is represented by `ArrayBuff ers`, but it can also be represented by `SharedArrayBuffers`. In addition, there are WebAssembly instructions for atomic operations, similar to the `Atomics` object we have in JavaScript. With `SharedArrayBuffers`, atomic operations, and web workers (or `worker_threads` in Node.js), we have enough to do the full suite of multithreaded programming tasks using WebAssembly.

Before we jump into multithreaded WebAssembly, let's build a "Hello, World!" example and execute it, to find the strengths and limitations of WebAssembly.

Your First WebAssembly

While WebAssembly is a binary format, a plain text format exists to represent it in human readable form. This is comparable to how machine code can by represented in a human-readable assembly language. The language for this WebAssembly text format is simply called WebAssembly text format, but the file extension typically used is *.wat*, so it's common enough to refer to this language as WAT. It uses *S-expressions* as its primary syntactic separator, which is helpful for both parsing and readability. S-expressions, known primarily from the Lisp family of languages, are nested lists delimited by parentheses, with whitespace between each item in the list.

To get a feel for this format, let's implement a simple addition function in WAT. Create a file called *ch7-wasm-add/add.wat* and add the contents of Example 7-1.

Example 7-1. ch7-wasm-add/add.wat

```
(module ❶
  (func $add (param $a i32) (param $b i32) (result i32) ❷
    local.get $a ❸
    local.get $b
    i32.add)
  (export "add" (func $add)) ❹
)
```

❶   The first line declares a module. Every WAT file begins with this.

❷   We declare a function called $add, taking in two 32-bit integers and returning another 32-bit integer.

❸   This is the start of the function body, in which we have three statements. The first two grab the function parameters and put them on the stack one after another. Recall that WebAssembly is stack-based. That means many operations will operate on the first (if unary) or first two (if binary) items on the stack. The third statement is a binary "add" operation on i32 values, so it grabs the top two values from the stack and adds them together, putting the result at the top of the stack. The return value for a function is the value at the top of the stack once it completes.

❹   In order to use a function outside the module in the host environment, it needs to be exported. Here we export the $add function, giving it the external name add.

We can convert this WAT file to WebAssembly binary by using the wat2wasm tool from the WebAssembly Binary Toolkit (WABT). This can be done with the following one-liner in the *ch7-wasm-add* directory.

```
$ npx -p wabt wat2wasm add.wat -o add.wasm
```

Now we have our first WebAssembly file! These files aren't useful outside a host environment, so let's write a bit of JavaScript to load the WebAssembly and test the add function. Add the contents of Example 7-2 to *ch7-wasm-add/add.js*.

Example 7-2. ch7-wasm-add/add.js

```
const fs = require('fs/promises'); // Needs Node.js v14 or higher.

(async () => {
  const wasm = await fs.readFile('./add.wasm');
  const { instance: { exports: { add } } } = await WebAssembly.instantiate(wasm);
  console.log(add(2, 3));
})();
```

Provided you've created the *.wasm* file using the preceding wat2wasm command, you should be able to run this in the *ch7-wasm-add* directory.

```
$ node add.js
```

You can verify from the output that we are, in fact, adding via our WebAssembly module.

Simple mathematical operations on the stack don't make any use of linear memory or of concepts that have no meaning in WebAssembly, such as strings. Consider strings in C. Effectively, they're nothing more than a pointer to the start of an array of bytes, terminated by a null byte. We can't pass whole arrays by value to WebAssembly functions or return them, but we can pass them by reference. This means that to pass a string as an argument, we need to first allocate the bytes in the linear memory and write to them, then pass the index of the first byte to the WebAssembly function. This can get more complex since we then need ways of managing the available space in the linear memory. We basically need malloc() and free() implementations operating on the linear memory.[1]

Hand-writing WebAssembly in WAT, while clearly possible, isn't usually the easiest path to being productive and getting performance gains with it. It was designed to be a compile target for higher-level languages, and that's where it really shines. "Compiling C Programs to WebAssembly with Emscripten" on page 159 explores that in more detail.

Atomic Operations in WebAssembly

Although a full treatment of every WebAssembly instruction (*https://oreil.ly/PfxJq*) would be out of place in this book, it's worth pointing out the instructions specific to atomic operations on shared memory since they're key to multithreaded WebAssembly code, whether compiled from another language or hand-written in WAT.

---

1 In C and other languages without automatic memory management, memory must be allocated for use with allocation functions like malloc() and then freed for later allocation with functions like free(). Memory management techniques like garbage collection make it easier to write programs in higher-level languages like JavaScript, but they aren't a built-in feature of WebAssembly.

WebAssembly instructions often start with the type. In the case of atomic operations, the type is always `i32` or `i64`, corresponding to 32-bit and 64-bit integers, respectively. All atomic operations have `.atomic.` next in the instruction name. After that, you'll find the specific instruction name.

Let's go over some of the atomic operation instructions. We won't go over exact syntax, but this should give you an idea of the kinds of operations available at the instruction level:

`[i32|i64].atomic.[load|load8_u|load16_u|load32_u]`
> The `load` family of instructions is equivalent to `Atomics.load()` in JavaScript. Using one of the suffixed instructions allows you to load smaller numbers of bits, extending the result with zeros.

`[i32|i64].atomic.[store|store8|store16|store32]`
> The `store` family of instructions is equivalent to `Atomics.store()` in JavaScript. Using one of the suffixed instructions wraps the input value to that number of bits and stores those at the index.

`[i32|i64].atomic.[rmw|rmw8|rmw16|rmw32].[add|sub|and|or|xor|xchg|cmpxchg][|_u]`
> The `rmw` family of instructions all perform read-modify-write operations, equivalent to `add()`, `sub()`, `and()`, `or()`, `xor()`, `exchange()`, and `compareExchange()` from the `Atomics` object in JavaScript, respectively. The operations are suffixed with a `_u` when they zero-extend, and `rmw` can have a suffix corresponding to the number of bits to be read.

The next two operations have a slightly different naming convention:

`memory.atomic.[wait32|wait64]`
> These are equivalent to `Atomics.wait()` in JavaScript, suffixed according to the number of bits they operate on.

`memory.atomic.notify`
> This is equivalent to `Atomics.notify()` in JavaScript.

These instructions are enough to perform the same atomic operations in WebAssembly as we can in JavaScript, but there is an additional operation not available in JavaScript:

`atomic.fence`
> This instruction takes no arguments and doesn't return anything. It's intended to be used by higher-level languages that have ways of guaranteeing ordering of nonatomic accesses to shared memory.

All of these operations are used with the given WebAssembly module's *linear memory*, which is the sandbox in which it gets to read and write values. When WebAssembly modules are initialized from JavaScript, they can be initialized with a linear memory provided as an option. This can be backed by a `SharedArrayBuffer` to enable usage across threads.

Although it's certainly possible to use these instructions in WebAssembly, they suffer from the same drawback that the rest of WebAssembly does: it's incredibly tedious and painstaking to write. Luckily, we can compile higher-level languages down to WebAssembly.

Compiling C Programs to WebAssembly with Emscripten

Since long before WebAssembly, Emscripten (*https://emscripten.org*) has been the go-to way to compile C and C++ programs for use in JavaScript environments. Today, it supports multithreaded C and C++ code using web workers in browsers and `worker_threads` in Node.js.

In fact, a large corpus of existing multithreaded code in the wild can be compiled with Emscripten without issue. In both Node.js and browsers, Emscripten emulates the system calls used by native code compiled to WebAssembly so that programs written in compiled languages can run without many changes.

Indeed, the C code we wrote way back in Chapter 1 can be compiled without any editing! Let's give that a try now. We'll use a Docker image to simplify using Emscripten. For other compiler toolchains, we'd want to make sure that the toolchain aligns with the system, but since WebAssembly and JavaScript are both platform-agnostic, we can just use the Docker image wherever Docker is supported.

First, make sure Docker is installed (*https://docker.com*). Then, in your *ch1-c-threads* directory, run the following command:

```
$ docker run --rm -v $(pwd):/src -u $(id -u):$(id -g) \
  emscripten/emsdk emcc happycoin-threads.c -pthread \
  -s PTHREAD_POOL_SIZE=4 -o happycoin-threads.js
```

There are a few things to discuss with this command. We're running the `emscripten/emsdk` image, with the current directory mounted, running as the current user. Everything after and including `emcc` is the command we're running inside the container. For the most part, this looks a lot like what we'd do when using `cc` to compile a C program. The main difference is that the output file is a JavaScript file rather than an executable binary. Don't worry! A *.wasm* file is also generated. The JS file is used as a bridge to any necessary system calls and to set up the threads because those can't be instantiated in WebAssembly alone.

The other extra argument is `-s PTHREAD_POOL_SIZE=4`. Since `happycoin-threads.c` uses three threads, we allocate them ahead of time here. There are a few ways to handle thread creation in Emscripten, largely due to not blocking on main browser threads. It's easiest to preallocate here since we know how many threads we'll need.

Now we can run our WebAssembly version of multithreaded Happycoin. We'll run the JavaScript file with Node.js. At time of writing, this requires Node.js v16 or higher, since that's what the output of Emscripten supports.

```
$ node happycoin-threads.js
```

The output should look a bit like the following:

```
120190845798210000 ... [ 106 more entries ] ... 14356375476580480000
count 108
Pthread 0x9017f8 exited.
Pthread 0x701500 exited.
Pthread 0xd01e08 exited.
Pthread 0xb01b10 exited.
```

The output looks the same as our other Happycoin examples from previous chapters, but the wrapper provided by Emscripten also informs us when the threads have exited. You'll also need to Ctrl+C to exit the program. For extra fun, see if you can figure out what needs changing in order to make the process exit when done, and avoid those `Pthread` messages.

One thing you may notice when comparing against the native or JavaScript versions of Happycoin is timing. It's clearly faster than the multithreaded JavaScript version, but also a bit slower than the native multithreaded C version. As always, it's important to take measurements of your application to ensure that you're getting the right benefits with the right trade-offs.

While the Happycoin example doesn't make use of any atomic operations, Emscripten supports the full suite of POSIX thread functionality and GNU Compiler Collection (GCC) built-in atomic operation functions. This means a great multitude of C and C++ programs can compile to WebAssembly using Emscripten.

Other WebAssembly Compilers

Emscripten isn't the only way to compile code to WebAssembly. Indeed, WebAssembly was designed primarily as a compile target, rather than as a general-purpose language in its own right. There are myriad tools for compiling well-known languages to WebAssembly, and there are even some languages built with WebAssembly as the main target in mind, rather than machine code. Some are listed here, but it's by no means exhaustive (*https://oreil.ly/wKfBe*). You'll notice a lot of "at time of writing" here, because this space is relatively new and the best ways of creating multithreaded WebAssembly code are still being developed! At least, at time of writing.

Clang/Clang++

The LLVM C-family compilers can target WebAssembly with the `-target wasm32-unknown-unknown` or `-target wasm64-unknown-unknown` options, respectively. This is actually what Emscripten is now based on, in which POSIX threads and atomic operations work as expected. At time of writing, this is some of the best support for multithreaded WebAssembly. While `clang` and `clang++` support WebAssembly output, the recommended approach is to use Emscripten, to get the full suite of platform support in browsers and Node.js.

Rust

The Rust programming language compiler `rustc` supports WebAssembly output. The Rust website is a great starting point (*https://oreil.ly/ibOs3*) on how to use `rustc` in this way. To make use of threads, you can use the `wasm-bindgen-rayon` crate (*https://oreil.ly/Pyuv4*), which provides a parallelism API implemented using web workers. At time of writing, Rust's standard library thread support won't work.

AssemblyScript

The AssemblyScript compiler takes a subset of TypeScript as input, then generates WebAssembly output. While it does not support spawning threads, it does support atomic operations and using `SharedArrayBuffers`, so as long as you handle the threads themselves on the JavaScript side via web workers or `worker_threads`, you can make full use of multithreaded programming in AssemblyScript. We'll cover it in more depth in the next section.

There are, of course, many more options, with new ones arriving all the time. It's worth having a look around the web to see if your compiled language of choice can target WebAssembly, and whether or not it supports atomic operations in WebAssembly.

AssemblyScript

AssemblyScript (*https://assemblyscript.org*) is a subset of TypeScript (*https://typescript lang.org*) that compiles to WebAssembly. Rather than compiling an existing langauge and providing implementations of existing system APIs, AssemblyScript was designed as a way to produce WebAssembly code with a much more familiar syntax than WAT. A major selling point of AssemblyScript is that many projects use TypeScript already, so adding some AssemblyScript code to take advantage of WebAssembly doesn't require as much of a context-switch or even learning an entirely different programming language.

An AssemblyScript module looks a lot like a TypeScript module. If you're unfamiliar with TypeScript, it can be thought of as ordinary JavaScript, but with some additional syntax to indicate type information. Here is a basic TypeScript module that performs addition:

```
export function add(a: number, b: number): number {
  return a + b
}
```

You'll notice this looks almost exactly the same as a plain ECMAScript module, with the exception of type information in the form of : number after each of the function arguments and identifying the return value's type. The TypeScript compiler can use these types to check that any code calling this function is passing in the correct types and assuming the correct type on the return value.

AssemblyScript looks much the same, except instead of using JavaScript's number type, there are built-in types for each of the WebAssembly types. If we wanted to write the same addition module in TypeScript, and assuming 32-bit integers everywhere for types, it would look something like Example 7-3. Go ahead and add that to a file called *ch7-wasm-add/add.ts*.

Example 7-3. ch7-wasm-add/add.ts

```
export function add(a: i32, b: i32): i32 {
  return a + b
}
```

Since AssemblyScript files are just TypeScript, they use the *.ts* extension just the same. To compile a given AssemblyScript file to WebAssembly, we can use the asc command from the assemblyscript module. Try running the following command in the *ch7-wasm-add* directory:

```
$ npx -p assemblyscript asc add.ts --binaryFile add.wasm
```

You can try running the WebAssembly code using the same *add.js* file from Example 7-2. The output should be the same since the code is the same.

If you omit the --binaryFile add.wasm you'll get the module as translated into WAT, as shown in Example 7-4. You'll see it's roughly the same as Example 7-1.

Example 7-4. The WAT rendition of the AssemblyScript add function

```
(module
 (type $i32_i32_=>_i32 (func (param i32 i32) (result i32)))
 (memory $0 0)
 (export "add" (func $add/add))
 (export "memory" (memory $0))
 (func $add/add (param $0 i32) (param $1 i32) (result i32)
  local.get $0
  local.get $1
```

```
    i32.add
 )
)
```

AssemblyScript doesn't provide the ability to spawn threads, but threads can be spawned in the JavaScript environment, and `SharedArrayBuffers` can be used for the WebAssembly memory. Most importantly, it supports atomic operations via a global `atomics` object, not particularly different from regular JavaScript's `Atomics`. The main difference is that rather than operating on a `TypedArray`, these functions operate on the linear memory of the WebAssembly module, with a pointer and an optional offset. See the AssemblyScript documentation (*https://oreil.ly/LhTkW*) for details.

To see this in action, let's create one more implementation of our Happycoin example that we've been iterating on since Chapter 1.

Happycoin in AssemblyScript

Much like previous versions of our Happycoin example, this approach multiplexes the crunching of numbers over several threads and sends the results back. It's a glimpse of how multithreaded AssemblyScript can work. In a real-world application, you'd want to take advantage of shared memory and atomic operations, but to keep things simple, we'll stick with just fanning the work out to the threads.

Let's begin by creating a directory called *ch7-happycoin-as* and switch to that directory. We'll initialize a new project and add some necessary dependencies as follows:

```
$ npm init -y
$ npm install assemblyscript
$ npm install @assemblyscript/loader
```

The `assemblyscript` package includes the AssemblyScript compiler, and the `assemblyscript/loader` package gives us handy tools for interacting with the built module.

In the `scripts` object in the newly created *package.json*, we'll add `"build"` and `"start"` properties to simplify the compilation and running of the program:

```
"build": "asc happycoin.ts --binaryFile happycoin.wasm --exportRuntime",
"start": "node --no-warnings --experimental-wasi-unstable-preview1 happycoin.mjs"
```

The additional `--exportRuntime` parameter gives us some high-level tools for interacting with values from AssemblyScript. We'll get into that a bit later.

When invoking Node.js in the `"start"` script, we pass the experimental WASI flag. This enables the WebAssembly System Interface (WASI) (*https://wasi.dev*) interface, giving WebAssembly access to system-level functionality that would otherwise be inaccessible. We'll use this from AssemblyScript to generate random numbers.

Because it's experimental at time of writing, we'll add the `--no-warnings` flag[2] to suppress the warning we get for using WASI. The experimental status also means the flag may change in the future, so always be sure to consult the Node.js documentation for the version of Node.js you're running.

Now, let's write some AssemblyScript! Example 7-5 contains an AssemblyScript version of the Happycoin algorithm. Go ahead and add it to a file called *happycoin.ts*.

Example 7-5. ch7-happycoin-as/happycoin.ts

```
import 'wasi'; ❶

const randArr64 = new Uint64Array(1);
const randArr8 = Uint8Array.wrap(randArr64.buffer, 0, 8); ❷
function random64(): u64 {
  crypto.getRandomValues(randArr8); ❸
  return randArr64[0];
}

function sumDigitsSquared(num: u64): u64 {
  let total: u64 = 0;
  while (num > 0) {
    const numModBase = num % 10;
    total += numModBase ** 2;
    num = num / 10;
  }
  return total;
}

function isHappy(num: u64): boolean {
  while (num != 1 && num != 4) {
    num = sumDigitsSquared(num);
  }
  return num === 1;
}

function isHappycoin(num: u64): boolean {
  return isHappy(num) && num % 10000 === 0;
}

export function getHappycoins(num: u32): Array<u64> {
  const result = new Array<u64>();
  for (let i: u32 = 1; i < num; i++) {
    const randomNum = random64();
    if (isHappycoin(randomNum)) {
      result.push(randomNum);
```

---

2 In general, this isn't a flag you want to have enabled for a production application. Hopefully by the time you read this, WASI support will no longer be experimental. If that's the case, adjust these arguments accordingly.

```
    }
  }
  return result;
}
```

❶ The `wasi` module is imported here to ensure that the appropriate WASI-enabled globals are loaded.

❷ We initialized a `Uint64Array` for our random numbers, but `crypto.getRandom Values()` only works with `Uint8Array`, so we'll create one of those here as a view on the same buffer. Also, the `TypedArray` constructors in AssemblyScript aren't overloaded, so instead there's a static `wrap()` method available to construct new `TypedArray` instances from `ArrayBuffer` instances.

❸ This method is the one we enabled WASI for.

If you're familiar with TypeScript, you might be thinking this file looks very close to just being a TypeScript port of "Happycoin: Revisited" on page 60. You'd be correct! This is one of the major advantages of AssemblyScript. We're not writing in a brand-new language, and yet we're writing code that maps very closely to WebAssembly. Note that the return value of the exported function is of type `Array<u64>`. Exported functions in WebAssembly can't return arrays of any kind, but they can return an index into the module's memory (a pointer, really), which is exactly what's happening here. We could deal with this manually, but as we'll see, the AssemblyScript loader makes it much easier.

Of course, since AssemblyScript doesn't provide a way of spawning threads on its own, we'll need to do that from JavaScript. For this example, we'll use ECMAScript modules to take advantage of top-level `await`, so go ahead and put the contents of Example 7-6 into a file called *happycoin.mjs*.

Example 7-6. ch7-happycoin-as/happycoin.mjs

```
import { WASI } from 'wasi'; ❶
import fs from 'fs/promises';
import loader from '@assemblyscript/loader';
import { Worker, isMainThread, parentPort } from 'worker_threads';

const THREAD_COUNT = 4;

if (isMainThread) {
  let inFlight = THREAD_COUNT;
  let count = 0;
  for (let i = 0; i < THREAD_COUNT; i++) {
    const worker = new Worker(new URL(import.meta.url)); ❷
    worker.on('message', msg => {
```

```
      count += msg.length;
      process.stdout.write(msg.join(' ') + ' ');
      if (--inFlight === 0) {
        process.stdout.write('\ncount ' + count + '\n');
      }
    });
  }
} else {
  const wasi = new WASI();
  const importObject = { wasi_snapshot_preview1: wasi.wasiImport };
  const wasmFile = await fs.readFile('./happycoin.wasm');
  const happycoinModule = await loader.instantiate(wasmFile, importObject);
  wasi.start(happycoinModule);

  const happycoinsWasmArray =
    happycoinModule.exports.getHappycoins(10_000_000/THREAD_COUNT);
  const happycoins = happycoinModule.exports.__getArray(happycoinsWasmArray);
  parentPort.postMessage(happycoins);
}
```

❶   This can't be done without the --experimental-wasi-unstable-preview1 flag.

❷   If you're new to ESM, this might look strange. We don't get the __filename variable available to us like we do in CommonJS modules. Instead the import.meta.url property gives us the full path as a file URL string. We need to pass that to the URL constructor for it to be usable as an input to the Worker constructor.

Adapted from "Happycoin: Revisited" on page 60, we're again checking whether we're in the main thread or not, and spawning four worker threads from the main thread. In the main thread, we're expecting only one message on the default MessagePort, containing an array of found Happycoins. We simply log those and a count of all of them once all the worker threads have sent the message.

On the else side, in the worker threads, we initialize a WASI instance to pass to the WebAssembly module, and then instantiate the module using @assemblyscript/ loader, giving us what we need to handle the array return value we get from the getHappycoins function. We call the getHappycoins() method exported by the module, which gives us a pointer to an array in the WebAssembly linear memory. The __getArray function, provided by the loader, converts that pointer into a JavaScript array, which we can then use as normal. We pass that to the main thread for output.

To run this example, run the following two commands. The first will compile the AssemblyScript to WebAssembly, and the second will run it via the JavaScript we just put together:

```
$ npm run build
$ npm start
```

The output will look roughly the same as with previous Happycoin examples. Here is the output from one local run:

```
7641056713284760000 ... [ 134 more entries ] ... 10495060512882410000
count 136
```

As with all of these solutions, it's important to evaluate the trade-offs made with proper benchmarks. As an exercise, try timing this example against the other Happycoin implementations in this book. Is it faster or slower? Can you figure out why? What improvements can be made?

Analysis

By now you should be pretty familiar with building multithreaded applications using JavaScript, whether it be code that runs in a user's browser or your server, or even applications that employ both. And, while this book provides a lot of use cases and reference material, at no point did it say "you should add multithreading to your application," and there's an important reason for this.

By and large the main reason to add workers to an application is to increase performance. But this trade-off comes with a cost of added complexity. The *KISS principle*, meaning "Keep It Simple, Stupid," suggests that your applications should be so stupidly simple that anyone can quickly look at the code and get an understanding of it. Being able to read code after it has been written is of paramount importance and simply adding threads to a program without purpose is an absolute violation of KISS.

There are absolutely good reasons to add threads to an application, and as long as you're measuring performance and confirming that speed gains outweigh added maintenance costs, then you've found yourself a situation deserving of threads. But how do you identify situations where threads will or will not help without going through all the work of implementing them? And how do you go about measuring performance impact?

When Not to Use

Threading is not a magic bullet capable of solving an application's performance problems. It is usually not the lowest-hanging fruit when it comes to performance, either, and should often be done as a final effort. This is particularly true in JavaScript, where multithreading isn't as widely understood by the community as other languages. Adding threading support may require heavy changes to an application, which means your effort-to-performance gains will likely be higher if you first hunt down other code inefficiencies first.

Once that's done, and you've made your application performant in other areas, you are then left with the question, "Is now a good time to add multithreading?" The rest of this section contains some situations where adding threads will most likely not provide any performance benefits. This can help you avoid going through some of the discovery work.

Low Memory Constraints

There is some additional memory overhead incurred when instantiating multiple threads in JavaScript. This is because the browser needs to allocate additional memory for the new JavaScript environment—this includes things like globals and APIs available to your code as well as under-the-hood memory used by the engine itself. This overhead might prove to be minimal in a normal server environment in the case of Node.js or a beefy laptop in the case of browsers. But it could be a hindrance if you're running code on an embedded ARM device with 512 MB of RAM or donated netbooks in a K–12 classroom.

What's the memory impact of additional threads? It's a little hard to quantify, and it changes depending on the JavaScript engine and platform. The safe answer is that, like most performance aspects, you should measure it in a real-world environment. But we can certainly try to get some concrete numbers.

First, let's consider a dead simple Node.js program that just kicks off a timer and doesn't pull in any third-party modules. This program looks like the following:

```
#!/usr/bin/env node

const { Worker } = require('worker_threads');
const count = Number(process.argv[2]) || 0;

for (let i = 0; i < count; i++) {
  new Worker(__dirname + '/worker.js');
}

console.log(`PID: ${process.pid}, ADD THREADS: ${count}`);
setTimeout(() => {}, 1 * 60 * 60 * 1000);
```

Running the program and measuring memory usage looks like this:

```
# Terminal 1
$ node leader.js 0
# PID 10000

# Terminal 2
$ pstree 10000 -pa # Linux only
$ ps -p 10000 -o pid,vsz,rss,pmem,comm,args
```

The `pstree` command displays the threads used by the program. It displays the main V8 JavaScript thread, as well as some of the background threads covered in "Hidden Threads" on page 9. Here is an example output from the command:

```
node,10000 ./leader.js
  ├─{node},10001
  ├─{node},10002
  ├─{node},10003
  ├─{node},10004
  ├─{node},10005
  └─{node},10006
```

The `ps` command displays information about the process, notably the memory usage of the process. Here's an example of the output from the command:

```
  PID    VSZ   RSS %MEM COMMAND    COMMAND
66766 1409260 48212  0.1 node      node ./leader.js
```

There are two important variables here used to measure the memory usage of a program, both of them measured in kilobytes. The first here is VSZ, or *virtual memory size*, which is the memory the process can access including swapped memory, allocated memory, and even memory used by shared libraries (such as TLS), approximately 1.4 GB. The next is RSS, or *resident set size*, which is the amount of physical memory currently being used by the process, approximately 48 MB.

Measuring memory can be a little hand wavy, and it's tricky to estimate how many processes can actually fit in memory. In this case, we'll mostly be looking at the RSS value.

Now, let's consider a more complicated version of the program using threads. Again, the same dead simple timer will be used, but in this case there will be a total of four threads created. In this case a new *worker.js* file is required:

```
console.log(`WPID: ${process.pid}`);
setTimeout(() => {}, 1 * 60 * 60 * 1000);
```

Running the *leader.js* program with a numerical argument greater than 0 allows the program to create additional workers. Table 8-1 is a listing of the memory usage output from `ps` for each of the different iterations of additional threads.

Table 8-1. Thread memory overhead with Node.js v16.5

Add Threads	VSZ	RSS	SIZE
0	318,124 KB	31,836 KB	47,876 KB
1	787,880 KB	38,372 KB	57,772 KB
2	990,884 KB	45,124 KB	68,228 KB
4	1,401,500 KB	56,160 KB	87,708 KB
8	2,222,732 KB	78,396 KB	126,672 KB
16	3,866,220 KB	122,992 KB	205,420 KB

Figure 8-1 displays the correlation between RSS memory and thread count.

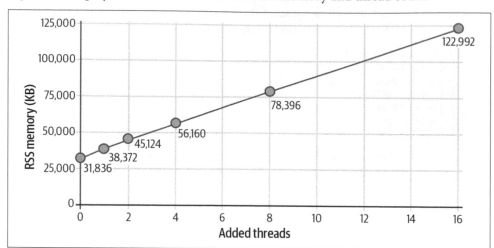

Figure 8-1. Memory usage increases with each additional thread

With this information it appears that the added RSS memory overhead of instantiating each new thread, using Node.js 16.5 on an x86 processor, is approximately 6 MB. Again, this number is a bit hand wavy, and you'll need to measure it in your particular situation. Of course, the memory overhead is compounded when the threads pull in more modules. If you were to instantiate heavy frameworks and web servers in each thread you may end up adding hundreds of megabytes of memory to your process.

 While it's becoming increasingly rare to find them, programs running on a 32-bit computer or smart phone have a maximum addressable memory space of 4 GB. This limit is shared across any threads in the program.

Low Core Count

Your application will run slower in situations where it has fewer cores. This is especially true if the machine has a single core, and it can also be true if it has two cores. Even if you employ a thread pool in your application and scale the pool based on the core count, the application will be slower if it creates a single worker thread. When creating an additional thread, the application now has at least two threads (the main and the worker), and the two threads will compete with each other for attention.

Another reason your application will slow down is that there is additional overhead when it comes to communicating between threads. With a single core and two threads, even if the two never compete for resources, i.e., the main thread has no work to do while the worker is running and vice versa, there is still an overhead when performing message passing between the two threads.

This might not be a huge deal. For example, if you create a distributable application that runs in many environments, often running on multicore systems and infrequently on single-core systems, then this overhead might be OK. But if you're building an application that almost entirely runs in a single-core environment, you would likely be better off by not adding threading at all. That is, you probably shouldn't build an app that takes advantage of your beefy multicore developer laptop and then ship it to production where a container orchestrator limits the app to a single core.

How much of a performance loss are we talking? On the Linux operating system it's straightforward to tell the OS that a program, and all of its threads, should only run on a subset of CPU cores. The use of this command allows developers to test the effects of running a multithreaded application in a low core environment. If you're using a Linux-based computer, then feel free to run these examples; if not, a summary will be provided.

First, go back to the *ch6-thread-pool/* example that you created in "Thread Pool" on page 121. Execute the application so that it creates a worker pool with two workers:

```
$ THREADS=2 STRATEGY=leastbusy node main.js
```

Note that with a thread pool of 2, the application has three JavaScript environments available, and libuv should have a default pool of 5, leading to a total of about eight threads as of Node.js v16. With the program running and able to access all of the cores on your machine, you're ready to run a quick benchmark. Execute the following command to send a barrage of requests to the server:

```
$ npx autocannon http://localhost:1337/
```

In this case we're just interested in the average request rate, identified in the last table of the output with the Req/Sec row and the Avg column. In one sample run the value of 17.5 was returned.

Kill the server with Ctrl+C and run it again. But this time use the `taskset` command to force the process (and all of its child threads) to use the same CPU core:

```
# Linux only command
$ THREADS=2 STRATEGY=leastbusy taskset -c 0 node main.js
```

In this case the two environment variables THREADS and STRATEGY are set, then the `taskset` command is run. The `-c 0` flag tells the command to only allow the program to use the 0th CPU. The arguments that follow are then treated as the command to run. Note that the `taskset` command can also be used to modify an already running process. When that happens the command displays some useful output to tell you what happens. Here's a copy of that output when the command is used on a computer with 16 cores:

```
pid 211154's current affinity list: 0-15
pid 211154's new affinity list: 0
```

In this case it says that the program used to have access to all 16 cores (0–15), but now it only has access to one (0).

With the program running and locked to a single CPU core to emulate an environment with fewer cores available, run the same benchmark command again:

```
$ npx autocannon http://localhost:1337/
```

In one such run the average requests per second has been reduced to 8.32. This means that the throughput of this particular program, when trying to use three JavaScript threads in a single-core environment, leads to a performance of 48% when compared to having access to all cores!

A natural question might be: in order to maximize the throughput of the *ch6-thread-pool* application, how large should the thread pool be and how many cores should be provided to the application? To find an answer, 16 permutations of the benchmark were applied to the application and the performance was measured. The length of the test was doubled to two minutes to help reduce any outlying requests. A tabular version of this data is provided in Table 8-2.

Table 8-2. Available cores versus thread pool size and how it affects throughput

	1 core	2 cores	3 cores	4 cores
1 thread	8.46	9.08	9.21	9.19
2 threads	8.69	9.60	17.61	17.28
3 threads	8.23	9.38	16.92	16.91
4 threads	8.47	9.57	17.44	17.75

A graph of the data has been reproduced in Figure 8-2.

In this case there is an obvious performance benefit when the number of threads dedicated to the thread pool is at least two and the number of cores available to the application is at least three. Other than that, there isn't anything too interesting about the data. When measuring the effects of cores versus threads in a real-world application, you will likely see more interesting performance trade-offs.

One question posed by this data is: why doesn't adding more than two threads or three threads make the application any faster? Answering questions like these will require hypotheses, experimenting with application code, and trying to erase any bottlenecks. In this case it may be that the main thread is so busy coordinating, handling requests, and communicating with threads, that the worker threads aren't able to get much work done.

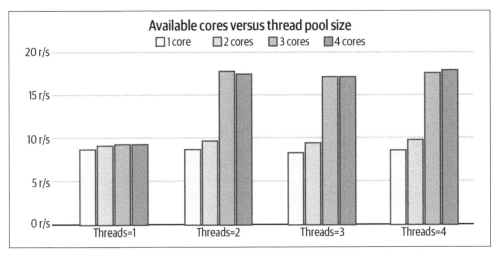

Figure 8-2. Available cores versus thread pool size and how it affects throughput

Containers Versus Threads

When it comes to writing server software, like with Node.js, the rule of thumb is that processes should scale horizontally. This is a fancy term meaning you should run multiple redundant versions of the program in an isolated manner—such as within a Docker container. Horizontal scaling benefits performance in a way that allows developers to fine-tune the performance of the whole fleet of applications. Such tuning can't be performed as easily when the scaling primitive happens within the program, in the form of a thread pool.

Orchestrators, such as Kubernetes, are tools that run containers across multiple servers. They make it easy to scale an application on demand; during the holiday season an engineer can manually increase the number of instances running. Orchestrators can also dynamically change the scale depending on other heuristics like CPU usage, traffic throughput, and even the size of a work queue.

How might this dynamic scaling look if it were performed within an application at runtime? Well, certainly the available thread pool would need to be resized. There would also need to be some sort of communication in place, allowing an engineer to send messages to the processes to resize the pool; perhaps an additional server needs to listen on a port for such administrative commands. Such functionality then requires additional complexity to be added to the application code.

While adding additional processes instead of increasing thread count increases overall resource consumption, not to mention the overhead of wrapping processes in a container, larger companies usually prefer the scaling flexibility of this approach.

When to Use

Sometimes you'll get lucky and will end up with a problem that benefits greatly from a multithreaded solution. Here are some of the most straightforward characteristics of such a problem to keep an eye out for:

Embarrassingly parallel

This is a class of problems where a large task can be broken down into smaller tasks and very little or no sharing of state is required. One such problem is the Game of Life simulation covered in "Example Application: Conway's Game of Life" on page 106. With that problem, the game grid can be subdivided into smaller grids, and each grid can be dedicated to an individual thread.

Heavy math

Another characteristic of problems that are a good fit for threads are those that involve a heavy use of math, aka CPU-intensive work. Sure, one might say that everything a computer does is math, but the inverse of a math-heavy application is one that is I/O heavy, or one that mostly deals with network operations. Consider a password hash cracking tool that has a weak SHA1 digest of a password. Such tools may work by running the Secure Hash Algorithm 1 (SHA1) algorithm over every possible combination of 10 character passwords, which is a lot of number crunching indeed.

MapReduce-friendly problems

MapReduce is a programming model that is inspired by functional programming. This model is often used for large-scale data processing that has been spread across many different machines. MapReduce is broken into two pieces. The first is Map, which accepts a list of values and produces a list of values. The second is Reduce, where the list of values are iterated on again, and a singular value is produced. A single-threaded version of this could be created in Java-Script using `Array#map()` and `Array#reduce()`, but a multithreaded version requires different threads processing subsets of the lists of data. A search engine uses Map to scan millions of documents for keywords, then Reduce to score and rank them, providing a user with a page of relevant results. Database systems like Hadoop and MongoDB benefit from MapReduce.

Graphics processing

A lot of graphics processing tasks also benefit from multiple threads. Much like the Game of Life problem, which operates on a grid of cells, images are represented as a grid of pixels. In both cases the value at each coordinate can be represented as a number, though Game of Life uses a single 1-bit number while images are more likely to use 3 or 4 bytes (red, green, blue, and optional alpha transparency). Image filtering then becomes a problem of subdividing an image into smaller images, having threads in a thread-pool process with the smaller images in parallel, then updating the interface once the change is complete.

This isn't a complete list of all the situations in which you should use multithreading; it's just a list of some of the most obvious use cases.

One of the repeating themes is that problems that don't require shared data, or at least that don't require coordinated reads and writes to shared data, are easier to model using multiple threads. Though it's generally beneficial to write code that doesn't have many side effects, this benefit is compounded when writing multithreaded code.

Another use case that's particularly beneficial to JavaScript applications is that of template rendering. Depending on the library used, the rendering of a template might be done using a string that represents the raw template and an object that contains variables to modify the template. With such use cases there usually isn't much global state to consider, just the two inputs, while a single string output is returned. This is the case with the popular template rendering packages `mustache` and `handlebars`. Offloading template rendering from the main thread of a Node.js application seems like a reasonable place to gain performance.

Let's test this assumption out. Create a new directory named *ch8-template-render/*. Inside this directory, copy and paste the existing *ch6-thread-pool/rpc-worker.js* file from Example 6-3. Although the file will work fine unmodified, you should comment out the `console.log()` statement so that it doesn't slow down the benchmark.

You'll also want to initialize an npm project and install some basic packages. You can do this by running the following commands:

```
$ npm init -y
$ npm install fastify@3 mustache@4
```

Next, create a file named *server.js*. This represents an HTTP application that performs basic HTML rendering when it receives a request. This benchmark is going to use some real-world packages instead of loading built-in modules for everything. Start the file off with the contents of Example 8-1.

Example 8-1. ch8-template-render/server.js (part 1)

```
#!/usr/bin/env node
// npm install fastify@3 mustache@4

const Fastify = require('fastify');
const RpcWorkerPool = require('./rpc-worker.js');
const worker = new RpcWorkerPool('./worker.js', 4, 'leastbusy');
const template = require('./template.js');
const server = Fastify();
```

The file starts off by instantiating the Fastify web framework, as well as a worker pool with four workers. The application also loads a module named *template.js* that will be used to render templates used by the web application.

Now, you're ready to declare some routes and to tell the server to listen for requests. Keep editing the file by adding the content from Example 8-2 to it.

Example 8-2. ch8-template-render/server.js (part 2)

```
server.get('/main', async (request, reply) =>
  template.renderLove({ me: 'Thomas', you: 'Katelyn' }));

server.get('/offload', async (request, reply) =>
  worker.exec('renderLove', { me: 'Thomas', you: 'Katelyn' }));

server.listen(3000, (err, address) => {
  if (err) throw err;
  console.log(`listening on: ${address}`);
});
```

Two routes have been introduced to the application. The first is GET /main and will perform the rendering of the request in the main thread. This represents a single-threaded application. The second route is GET /offload, where the rendering work will be offloaded to a separate worker thread. Finally, the server is instructed to listen on port 3000.

At this point the application is functionally complete. But as an added bonus, it would be nice to be able to quantify the amount of work that the server is busy doing. While it's true that we can primarily test the efficiency of this application by using an HTTP request benchmark, sometimes it's nice to look at other numbers as well. Add the content from Example 8-3 to finish off the file.

Example 8-3. ch8-template-render/server.js (part 3)

```
const timer = process.hrtime.bigint;
setInterval(() => {
  const start = timer();
  setImmediate(() => {
    console.log(`delay: ${(timer() - start).toLocaleString()}ns`);
  });
}, 1000);
```

This code uses a setInterval call that runs every second. It wraps a setImmediate() call, measuring current time in nanoseconds before and after the call is made. It's not perfect, but it is one way to approximate how much load the process is currently receiving. As the event loop for the process gets busier, the number that is reported will get higher. Also, the busyness of the event loop affects the delay of asynchronous operations throughout the process. Keeping this number lower therefore correlates to a more performant application.

Next, create a file named *worker.js*. Add the content from Example 8-4 to it.

Example 8-4. ch8-template-render/worker.js

```
const { parentPort } = require('worker_threads');
const template = require('./template.js');

function asyncOnMessageWrap(fn) {
  return async function(msg) {
    parentPort.postMessage(await fn(msg));
  }
}

const commands = {
  renderLove: (data) => template.renderLove(data)
};

parentPort.on('message', asyncOnMessageWrap(async ({ method, params, id }) => ({
  result: await commands[method](...params), id
})));
```

This is a modified version of the worker file that you created before. In this case a single command is used, `renderLove()`, which accepts an object with key value pairs to be used by the template rendering function.

Finally, create a file named *template.js*, and add the content from Example 8-5 to it.

Example 8-5. ch8-template-render/template.js

```
const Mustache = require('mustache');
const love_template = "<em>{{me}} loves {{you}}</em> ".repeat(80);

module.exports.renderLove = (data) => {
  const result = Mustache.render(love_template, data);
  // Mustache.clearCache();
  return result;
};
```

In a real-world application, this file might be used for reading template files from disk and substituting values, exposing a complete list of templates. For this simple example just a single template renderer is exported and a single hard-coded template is used. This template uses two variables, me and you. The string is repeated many times to approach the length of a template that a real application might use. The longer the template, the longer it takes to render.

Now that the files have been created, you're ready to run the application. Run the following commands to run the server and then to launch a benchmark against it:

```
# Terminal 1
$ node server.js

# Terminal 2
$ npx autocannon -d 60 http://localhost:3000/main
$ npx autocannon -d 60 http://localhost:3000/offload
```

On a test run on a beefy 16-core laptop, when rendering templates entirely in the main thread, the application had an average throughput of 13,285 requests per second. However, when running the same test while offloading template rendering to a worker thread, the average throughput was 18,981 requests per second. In this particular situation it means the throughput increased by about 43%.

The event loop latency also decreased significantly. Sampling the time it takes to call `setImmediate()` while the process is idle gets us about 87 μs on average. When performing template rendering in the main thread, the latency averages 769 μs. The same samples taken when offloading rendering to a worker thread are on average 232 μs. Subtracting out the idle state from both values means it's about a 4.7x improvement when using threads. Figure 8-3 compares these samples over time during the 60-second benchmark.

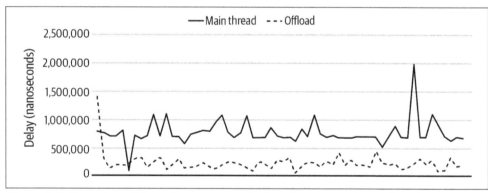

Figure 8-3. Event loop delay when using single thread versus multiple threads

Does this mean you should run out and refactor your applications to offload rendering to another thread? Not necessarily. With this contrived example the application was made faster with the additional threads, but this was done on a 16-core machine. It's very likely that your production applications have access to fewer cores.

That said, the biggest performance differentiator while testing this was the size of the templates. When they're a lot smaller, like without repeating the string, it's faster to render the templates in a single thread. The reason it's going to be slower is that the overhead of passing the template data between threads is going to be much larger than the time it takes to render a tiny template.

As with all benchmarks, take this one with a grain of salt. You'll need to test such changes with your application in a production environment to know for sure if it benefits from additional threads or not.

Summary of Caveats

This is a combined list of the aforementioned caveats when working with threads in JavaScript:

Complexity
Applications tend to be more complex when using shared memory. This is especially true if you are hand-writing calls with `Atomics` and manually working with `SharedBufferArray` instances. Now, admittedly, a lot of this complexity can be hidden from the application through the use of a third-party module. In such a case it can be possible to represent your workers in a clean manner, communicating with them from the main thread, and having all the intercommunication and coordination abstracted away.

Memory overhead
There is additional memory overhead with each thread that is added to a program. This memory overhead is compounded if a lot of modules are being loaded in each thread. Although the overhead might not be a huge deal on modern computers, it is worth testing on the end hardware the code will ultimately run on just to be safe. One way to help alleviate this issue is to audit the code that is being loaded in separate threads. Make sure you're not unnecessarily loading the kitchen sink!

No shared objects
The inability to share objects between threads can make it difficult to easily convert a single-threaded application to a multithreaded one. Instead, when it comes to mutating objects, you'll need to pass messages around that end up mutating an object that lives in a single location.

No DOM access
Only the main thread of a browser-based application has access to the DOM. This can make it difficult to offload UI rendering tasks to another thread. That said, it's entirely possible for the main thread to be in charge of DOM mutation while additional threads can do the heavy lifting and return data changes to the main thread to update the UI.

Modified APIs

Along the same lines as the lack of DOM access, there are slight changes to APIs available in threads. In the browser this means no calls to `alert()`, and individual worker types have even more rules, like disallowing blocking `XMLHttpRe quest#open()` requests, `localStorage` restrictions, top-level `await`, etc. While some concerns are a little fringe, it does mean that not all code can run unmodified in every possible JavaScript context. Documentation is your friend when dealing with this.

Structured clone algorithm constraints

There are some constraints on the structured clone algorithm that may make it difficult to pass certain class instances between different threads. Currently, even if two threads have access to the same class definition, instances of the class passed between threads become plain `Object` instances. While it's possible to rehydrate the data back into a class instance, it does require manual effort.

Browsers require special headers

When working with shared memory in the browser via `SharedArrayBuffer`, the server must supply two additional headers in the request for the HTML document used by the page. If you have complete control of the server, then these headers may be easy to introduce. However, in certain hosting environments, it might be difficult or impossible to supply such headers. Even the package used in this book to host a local server required modifications to enable the headers.

Thread preparedness detection

There is no built-in functionality to know when a spawned thread is ready to work with shared memory. Instead, a solution must first be built that essentially pings the thread and then waits until a response has been received.

Structured Clone Algorithm

The *structured clone algorithm* is a mechanism that JavaScript engines use when copying objects using certain APIs. Most notably, it's used when passing data between workers, though other APIs use it as well. With this mechanism, data is serialized and then later deserialized as an object inside another JavaScript realm.

When objects are cloned in this manner, such as from the main thread to a worker thread or from one worker to another, modifying an object on one side will not affect the object on the other side. There are essentially two copies of the data now. The purpose of the structured clone algorithm is to provide a friendlier mechanism for developers than what JSON.stringify does, while imposing reasonable limitations.

Browsers use the structured clone algorithm when copying data between web workers. Node.js, similarly, uses it when copying data between worker threads. Basically, when you see a .postMessage() call, data being passed in is cloned in this way. Browsers and Node.js follow the same rules, but they each support additional object instances that can be copied.

As a quick rule of thumb, any data that can be cleanly represented as JSON can be safely cloned in this manner. Sticking to data represented in this manner will certainly lead to very few surprises. That said, the structured clone algorithm supports several other types of data as well.

First off, all of the primitive data types available in JavaScript, with the exception of the Symbol type, can be represented. This includes the Boolean, null, undefined, Number, BigInt, and String types.

Instances of Array, Map, and Set, which are each used for storing collections of data, can also be cloned in this manner. Even ArrayBuffer, ArrayBufferView, and Blob instances, which store binary data, can be passed along.

Instances of some more complex objects, as long as they are quite universal and well understood, can also be passed through. This includes objects created using the `Boolean` and `String` constructor, `Date`, and even `RegExp` instances.[1]

On the browser side, more complex and lesser-known object instances like those for `File`, `FileList`, `ImageBitmap`, and `ImageData` can be cloned.

On the Node.js side, special object instances that can be copied over include `WebAssembly.Module`, `CryptoKey`, `FileHandle`, `Histogram`, `KeyObject`, `MessagePort`, `net.BlockList`, `net.SocketAddress`, and `X509Certificate`. Even instances of `ReadableStream`, `WritableStream`, and `TransformStream` can be copied.

Another notable difference that works with the structured clone algorithm, but doesn't work with JSON objects, is that recursive objects (those with nested properties that reference another property) can also be cloned. The algorithm is smart enough to stop serializing an object once it encounters a duplicate, nested object.

There are several shortcomings that may affect your implementations. First, a function cannot be cloned in this manner. Functions can be pretty complex things. For example, they have a scope available and can access variables declared outside of them. Passing something like that between realms wouldn't make a whole lot of sense.

Another missing feature, which will likely affect your implementations, is that DOM elements in the browser cannot be passed along. Does this mean that the work that a web worker performs can't be displayed to the user in the DOM? Absolutely not. Instead, you'll need to have a web worker return a value that the main JavaScript realm is then able to transform and display to the user. For example, if you were to calculate 1,000 iterations of `fibonacci` in a web worker, the numeric value could be returned, and the calling JavaScript code could then take that value and place it in the DOM.

Objects in JavaScript are fairly complex. Sometimes they can be created using the object literal syntax. Other times they can be created by instantiating a base class. And still other times they can be modified by setting property descriptors and setters and getters. When it comes to the structured clone algorithm, only the basic values of objects are retained.

Most notably, this means that, when you define a class of your own and pass an instance to be cloned, only the own properties of that instance will be cloned, and the resulting object will be an instance of `Object`. Properties defined in the prototype will not be cloned either. Even if you define `class Foo {}` both on the calling side and

---

[1] There is a small caveat with `RegExp` instances. They contain a `.lastIndex` property, which is used when running a regular expression multiple times over the same string to know where the expression last ended. This property is not passed along.

inside the web worker, the value will still be an instance of `Object`. This is because there's no real way to guarantee that both sides of the clone are dealing with the exact same `Foo` class.[2]

Certain objects will entirely refuse to be cloned. For example, if you try to pass `win dow` from the main thread to a worker thread, or if you try to return `self` in the opposite direction, you may receive one of the following errors, depending on the browser:

```
Uncaught DOMException: The object could not be cloned.
DataCloneError: The object could not be cloned.
```

There are some inconsistencies across JavaScript engines, so it's best to test your code in multiple browsers. For example, Chrome and Node.js support cloning `Error` instances, but Firefox currently does not.[3] The general rule of thumb is that JSON-compatible objects should never be a problem, but more complex data might be. For that reason, passing around simpler data is usually best.

---

2 There are proposals to allow serializing and deserializing class instances, such as "User-defined structured clone for JavaScript objects" (*https://oreil.ly/HZUyz*), so this restriction might not be permanent.

3 Firefox is planning on supporting this eventually. See "Allow structured cloning of native error types" (*https://oreil.ly/wT4NG*).

Index

A

ACID (atomicity, consistency, isolation, durability), 84
acquire() method, 134
activate event, 38
    handler function, 38
actor models, 144
    actors variable, 147
    client argument, 148
    example implementation, 146-154
    hot code loading, 153
    JavaScript and, 146
    main server process, 148
    message_id variable, 147
    patterns, 145
alert() function, 98
API (application programming interface)
    fetch(), 24
    indexedDB, 24, 40
    localStorage, 24
    location, 25
    modified, 182
    Node.js, 56
    service workers, 34
    WebSocket, 24
    XMLHttpRequest, 24
ArrayBuffer
    contents display, 81
    Grid class, 108
    Object, inheriting from, 80
    strings and, 94
    views and, 82
    WebAssembly, 155
arrays

    BigUint64Array, 61
    threads, declaring, 16
    TypedArray, 61
AssemblyScript, 161
    assemblyscript package, 163
    Happycoin, 163-167
    module, 161
    spawning threads, 163
    .ts file extension, 162
    wasi module, 165
asynchronous code, 2
atomicity, 84
    atomic operations, 84
    concerns, 88-90
    WebAssembly, 155, 157-159
Atomics object, 73, 85
    Atomics.and() method, 85
    Atomics.compareExchange() method, 86
    Atomics.exchange() method, 86
    Atomics.isLockFree() method, 86
    Atomics.load() method, 86
    Atomics.notify() method, 98, 99, 100, 105
    Atomics.or() method, 87
    Atomics.store() method, 87, 90
    Atomics.sub() method, 87
    Atomics.wait() method, 98, 105
    Atomics.waitAsync() method, 100
    Atomics.xor() method, 87
    buffers, direct array access, 90
    coordination and, 97-100
    events and, 118-120
    nondeterminism, 100-106
    return values, conversion and, 90
    TypedArray instance, 85

X

About the Authors

Thomas Hunter II has contributed to dozens of enterprise Node.js services and has worked for a company dedicated to securing Node.js. He has spoken at several conferences on Node.js and JavaScript, is JSNSD/JSNAD certified, and is an organizer of NodeSchool SF.

Bryan English is an open source JavaScript and Rust programmer and enthusiast and has worked on large enterprise systems, instrumentation, and application security. Currently he's a senior open source software engineer at Datadog. He's used Node.js both professionally and in personal projects since not long after its inception. He is also a Node.js core collaborator and has contributed to Node.js in many ways through several of its various working groups.

Colophon

The bird on the cover of *Multithreaded JavaScript* is a green-winged teal (*Anas crecca*). This duck is commonly found in northerly Canadian wetlands and boreal forests, though it will migrate much farther south throughout much of the rest of North America in the winter.

Breeding males have gray flanks and backs with yellow rear ends and green patches on their chestnut heads. Their name comes from the distinctive white-edged green speculum feathers. Female green-winged teals are light brown and look very similar to female mallards. The green-winged teal is the smallest dabbling duck in North America. They prefer shallow water and are often found resting on stumps or mudbanks.

A rather noisy species, male green-winged teals have clear whistles, while female birds have notable "quacks." They seek their food primarily on mudflats or shallow marshes, and eat seeds, stems, and leaves of aquatic and emergent vegetation. They are preyed upon by humans, skunks, red foxes, raccoons, crows, and magpies.

The green-winged teal's current conservation status is "Least Concern." Many of the animals on O'Reilly covers are endangered; all of them are important to the world.

The cover illustration is by Karen Montgomery, based on a black and white engraving from *British Birds*. The cover fonts are Gilroy Semibold and Guardian Sans. The text font is Adobe Minion Pro; the heading font is Adobe Myriad Condensed; and the code font is Dalton Maag's Ubuntu Mono.

O'REILLY®

There's much more
where this came from.

Experience books, videos, live online
training courses, and more from O'Reilly
and our 200+ partners—all in one place.

Learn more at oreilly.com/online-learning